The Life and Work of
DAVID G. BLYTHE

DAVID G. BLYTHE (self-portrait in pencil)
(Heber H. Blythe, East Liverpool, O.)

The Life and Work of David G. Blythe

DOROTHY MILLER

University of Pittsburgh Press

PRINTED IN THE UNITED STATES OF AMERICA

To
Ann Bingham

ACKNOWLEDGMENTS

In preparing this material I have had the assistance of a great many people. My thanks go, especially, to Dr. Percival Hunt for guidance in style and organization and to my mother and brother, Harbaugh, for their encouragement and interest.

I would like to thank, too, Mr. Millard E. Blythe of East Liverpool, O., Mrs. J. Harry Gorley of Uniontown, Pa., Mrs. Alfred E. Meyer, Sr. of New Smyrna Beach, Fla., Mr. Walter R. Hovey and Miss Virginia Lewis of the University of Pittsburgh Department of Fine Arts, Mr. Thomas Jarrett of the University of Pittsburgh, and Mr. John O'Connor, Jr. of Carnegie Institute for important information and suggestions. I am grateful to all the owners of Blythe paintings for their gracious co-operation in every way. Permission to reproduce paintings has been given by Mrs. J. Insley Blair, Tuxedo Park, N. Y.; Mrs. Lucien Patton, Ligonier, Pa.; Mr. Alexander Nimick, Sewickley, Pa.; Miss Mary Irwin, Mr. Heber Blythe, Mr. W. H. Vodrey, and Mr. A. E. Webber, East Liverpool, O.; Mrs. James D. Hailman, the Carnegie Institute, and the Duquesne Club, Pittsburgh, Pa.; Harry Shaw Newman Gallery, New York, N. Y.; Brooklyn Museum; Memorial Art Gallery, Rochester, N. Y.; National Baseball Hall of Fame and Museum, Inc., Cooperstown, N. Y.

Dorothy Miller

TABLE OF CONTENTS

LIST OF ILLUSTRATIONS

The Life and Work of
DAVID G. BLYTHE

Chapter One

FAMILY BACKGROUND – BOYHOOD
PITTSBURGH APPRENTICESHIP
NAVAL EXPERIENCES

THE SCOTTISH integrity and self-reliance and the Irish wit and gusto which characterized David Blythe in his life and painting were his by right of birth. In 1808, John Blythe, David Blythe's father, crossed from Perth, where he had been born twenty-nine years before, to northern Ireland. There he met and married an Irish girl, Susan Gilmour. Six sons were born to them; the fourth, born in 1815, they christened David Gilmour Blythe.

In 1811, John and Susan with two sons, Thomas, two years old, and James, eight months, set out for America. They landed at New York in June after eleven weeks at sea. They settled for a time in Caledonia, a Scottish community in New York State, and there their third son, John, was born, on February 8, 1812.

For the most part, David Blythe's family background can be told only in the broad outlines of dates and places, for few records of details remain. Courage and independence seem suggested by the determination of his parents to emigrate to America. One other clue to family character is given by an account of an incident at Caledonia, written on the flyleaf of the first volume of the *Encyclopedia Perthensis* in April, 1889, by Thomas Blythe:

These twenty-three volumes were brought from the City of Perth in Scotland by our father John Blythe and grandfather of the present owner, Heber H. Blythe, when he emigrated to Ireland in 1808 and from there to the United States in 1811—while residing in New York in 1812 the books came to the notice of one Wadsworth, an extensive landowner, who earnestly desired to own them and made large offers for them, among them, offered to give 160 acres of good land adjoining a small village (or the "Corners" as it was called in that day) and which "Corners" or village grew to be what is now the City of Rochester, N. Y. and the 160 acres the center of the city. Father set such a high value on them that no consideration would be an inducement to his parting with them. They were consoling to him through life, when fatigued by labor or wearied with other reading, his resort for a rest was the big books and which some of us can testify to his wisdom in so doing. When he left New York State in 1814 to come to Ohio, he with family and worldly wealth, shipped on a raft at Olean, N. Y. for Pittsburgh. The raft ran on an island and was broken up. The books were in a large chest with other valuables and was caught by an Indian a few miles below the wreck. They were thoroughly wet which accounts for the stains on the pages now and the original binding was damaged. He had to pay the Indian 10 Silver Dollars before he would give up the chest which was quite a consideration at that of script and shin plasters.

The Blythes stopped for awhile in Pittsburgh, and then set out on the river again, following the windings of the Ohio northward and westward. Just beyond the Pennsylvania border they pulled their raft ashore where Fall Run joins the river, near Wellsville, two miles or so below the present town of East Liverpool. It was during the Blythe's stay there that a fourth son, David, was born on May 9, 1815.

In search of larger quarters for their increasing family, John and Susan Blythe moved to Snodgrass, now known as the Kountz Place, a mile down the river. There for a few months they lived in an old house on the Stewart farm, while their land was cleared and a new log home built.

The next years were busy ones for the Blythes. After the birth of Andrew, in 1817, and William, in 1819, there were six sons to be fed, clothed, and taught. The land, sloping toward the river, had to be cultivated, and the new home made comfortable. The boys learned to do the chores of the farm, but other needs were not neglected. They went to the country school in the winter and to the frame Presbyterian Church on Sundays; time was set aside for reading the Bible and the poems of English and Scottish writers. Probably on special occasions the encyclopedias were brought out and the boys allowed to turn their pages carefully. Then, too, there were trying experiences and sometimes extra hard work. On January 23, 1823, the Blythes watched flames destroy their house as well as John Blythe's cooper shop and tools. The family set to work again, and by spring a new home was ready. There the sons grew up. Later several of them went away to live and work, but John and Susan stayed on in this house.

As David grew older he found that he could do more than milk the cows, fetch water from the spring shared with the Fisher farm, feed the chickens, help plow the fields, and recite the three R's. He could draw and whittle with unusual skill. He would entertain his brothers with sketches drawn in charcoal on the door of the storage shed next to the barn. His subjects then, as at the height of his career in Pittsburgh, were neighborhood people, tramps, peddlers, and itinerant journeymen. Stories are told that when he showed his sketches, he had an appreciative audience in Mrs. John Fisher, Mrs. James Gaston, Mrs. Nancy McKinnon, and other women of the community, who gathered at the Blythes for quilting bees. So it seems Blythe had early his interest in genre subjects. Genre was both his first and his best painting. To choose it was inherent in him; he turned to it instinctively, naturally, and simply. The style and spirit that went into the sketch of the itinerant cobbler, Henry David, on a shed door, and of a country peddler on a fragment of slate, were the same that were in the paintings of a horsemarket in Pittsburgh and of two tramps on the banks of the Allegheny.

David Blythe at sixteen was a tall, sturdy, lanky young man, restless in spirit and clever with his hands. He set out for Pittsburgh, forty miles away, where he became an apprentice to Joseph Woodwell. Woodwell had a good business on Third Street. He specialized in designing mouldings, mantelpieces, staircases, panelling, and furniture for the new homes of Pittsburgh merchants and industrialists. The young apprentice undoubtedly had a hand in the carving of many decorative objects, some of which may still exist but cannot be traced. The only example of Blythe's work of which there is positive record is an insurance badge, although the badge itself cannot be found. A newspaper of 1832 prints that Blythe, after only six months' apprenticeship, carved a badge for the Fireman's Insurance Company of Pittsburgh, from which castings were made and placed by the Company, usually beside or above the front door, on the homes of those insuring with it.

That Blythe had skills in other crafts than wood carving is suggested by another newspaper account of a few years later: "Mr. Woodwell's attention was first called to Mr. Blythe's peculiar forte—drawing—by a picture executed on the wall of the shop, which, in the language of that gentleman, was done in a style worthy of an artist." Mr. Woodwell's statement came true. None of the drawings which caused the comment exist today so far as is known.

Although Blythe's artistic skill was given some expression in his apprentice days, he had no chance for formal art training. Pittsburgh of the thirties was a vigorous stimulating little city, but hardly had culture enough to rouse a young artist and to train him, or to furnish much of a market for his paintings. It was too busy hacking away the wilderness, building boats and foundries, and selling supplies to the many moving westward through the Gateway. Yet Pittsburgh was not altogether barren territory; it had some contact with the art beyond its hills and woods. J. J. Audubon passed its way in 1817, and painted a portrait of Benjamin Page and other Pittsburghers. Somehow, the next year, Chester Harding caught the spark and painted portraits while working in Pittsburgh as a house painter. In 1833 he came back to the town, after charming Europe and the eastern American cities, to paint Harmar Denny, Pittsburgh's mayor. Blythe and other young artists were likely to know that an artist of Harding's reputation was in Pittsburgh. They may even have watched him paint and found out something of his technique and style. This is, of course, all conjecture.

Some art historians have tried to find the source of Blythe's portrait style in the possibility that he may have watched Thomas Sully paint. It is interesting to consider this possibility. Of the two thousand portraits painted by Sully, eight of them were of Pittsburghers; yet if Sully ever visited Pittsburgh no mention is made of the visit in the very complete biography of Sully by Edward Biddle and Mantle Fielding. It is conceivable, of course, that Blythe did see and that perhaps he studied some of these portraits after they were hung in the homes of their owners. Their owners unquestionably felt great pride in them since they were the work of a famous portrait painter. It is more likely, though, that the touches of Sully in some of Blythe's later portraits were transmitted through

James R. Lambdin, who had studied with Sully in Philadelphia and who, in 1828, established in Pittsburgh an art gallery and museum. Blythe may well have watched Lambdin at work. The *Pittsburgh Mercury* reported on November 10, 1830, that at Lambdin's Gallery of Fine Arts at the southwest corner of Market and Fourth, open 8:00 A.M. to 9:00 P.M., for five cents one could view Dunlap's "Calvary." Blythe clearly had access to the gallery, and perhaps to the studio.

An obscure painter known to posterity only as A. Bowman gives a possible source in tracing the influences of other artists on Blythe's style. During Blythe's apprentice days Bowman returned to Pittsburgh, in 1830, after studying under Sir Thomas Lawrence. Some critics profess to see a tinge of English style in Blythe's mature portraits. Bowman may have brought that influence.

Apparently a Mr. Beale maintained some kind of gallery, for the *Pittsburgh Daily Advocate and Advertiser* carried on March 21, 1834, an announcement of an exhibit of "splendid paintings at Mr. Beale's Long Room where the following would be displayed: *Belshazzar's Feast, Capuchin Chapel, Cain Meditating the Death of Abel, Interior of a Nunnery,* and *The Battle of New Orleans.*" The artists are not specified, but the titles suggest dramatic and romantic subjects.

By 1834, the center of the art life of Pittsburgh was beginning to shift to an art store recently established by a young man hardly older than Blythe, J. J. Gillespie. The artists of the town began to gather there to trade ideas. Blythe was among them, and the friendship between Gillespie and Blythe started then and lasted until Blythe's death, in 1865. This association was one of the strongest forces shaping Blythe's interests and style; in sketching in the art life of Pittsburgh as a backdrop to Blythe's development as an artist, it cannot be overemphasized.

After serving his apprenticeship with Joseph Woodwell, Blythe remained in Pittsburgh a fourth year. He worked as a house painter, a vocation which probably pleased little his restless and creative temperament. In 1835, he joined his brother John, a steamboat captain, and traveled down the Mississippi to New Orleans on his boat.

No paintings or sketches remain from this journey, but its significance in Blythe's life may have been great. Besides opening up to him a part of the country he had never seen, it gave him a chance to see some of the artists near St. Louis and farther down the river who were engaged in preliminary sketches for massive panoramas. This forerunner of the motion picture was fast becoming a popular art. Henry Lewis, John Rowson Smith, and John Banvard were busy laying plans for the great projects that were to bring them international fame. They were already working on canvases ten and twelve feet in height and thousands of feet in length. These must have occasioned considerable comment and excitement all along the river. Blythe may have caught at this time the desire to try this spectacular type of painting. Years later he was to do just such a painting, a project which marked a turning point in his life and work.

Nothing further is known of this Mississippi adventure, and it is not until the early summer of 1837 that it is possible to pick up the thread of Blythe's activities. In July of that year David Blythe hiked to New York where he enlisted in the United States Navy. Whether this was a patriotic gesture or an adventure undertaken in the spirit of restlessness is a matter of conjecture. Later events in his life proved him ardently patriotic; that he was restless and high strung there is no doubt. Perhaps, then, his decision to join the Navy was a combination of both these forces.

Blythe boarded the sloop to which he was assigned at the

Brooklyn Navy Yard. There is some doubt whether he was classified a "Landsman" or "Ship's Carpenter," but at any rate the ship set sail on August 2, 1837, with Blythe's name appearing on the ship's roll as No. 127.

Notes copied from the log of the "Ontario" are of interest because they give us hints of possible streams of culture that may have crossed Blythe's course. By following the route of the ship it is possible to reconstruct to some extent this period in Blythe's life and to imagine something of the experiences he must have had—the people he saw, the places he visited. They combine to form another vague but interesting fragment in the puzzle-pattern of Blythe's life.

On November 7, 1837, the ship touched at Matanza, and a fortnight later it docked at Havana. December 1 it was reported off Key Largo. It went next to St. Croix, which it reached on December 31. The ship called at St. Thomas on January 9, 1838. Eight days later it docked at Puerto Rico, then sailed to Pensacola, and on to St. John's. It reached Cuba February 11 and a week later was at Port Royal. April 13 found it at Vera Cruz. It remained in these waters during the summer and fall. In the winter months the "Ontario" moved northward, and from December 9 until January 7, 1839, it was anchored in the Port of Boston.

During the month that the ship was in harbor at Boston, Blythe may not have been free to spend much time ashore. Possibly he went no farther ashore than the water-front taverns. On the other hand, he may have wandered through the town. Thus, because there is so little to go on in reconstructing his life and in weaving the background of his art, it becomes worth while to suggest every possible bypath that led him to paint as he did, and to speculate upon every possible source of influence and inspiration. Only by doing this can one really understand Blythe's work.

It is extremely unlikely that a sailor from a ship anchored in the harbor was welcomed into the homes of well-to-do Bostonian patrons of art, where he could have seen foreign paintings and prints. Nor is it likely that he was received in the studios of Washington Allston and other leading painters of Boston. It is remotely possible that Blythe's wandering led him to Pearl Street, where he might have entered The Athenaeum. If so, he could have seen *Jacob at the Well* attributed to Titian, Harding's *Hannah Adams,* Stuart's *George Washington* and *Martha Washington,* Allston's *Benjamin West,* Murillo's *Holy Family,* a few paintings by West, Sully, Trumbull, Panini, Neagle, some engravings by Audubon, and sculpture by Crawford, Greenough, Power, Ball, and Frazee. Blythe may have seen an exhibit of Washington Allston's paintings at Harding's Gallery on School Street that year.

Possibly Blythe was most influenced in Boston by the work of David Claypool Johnston. Issues of Johnston's *Annual* were widely circulated in Boston from 1830 to 1849. These "Scraps" contained sketches of runaway horses, inebriated gentlemen —distorted figures, all drawn with a racy sense of humor which would have struck a response in Blythe.

Blythe may have seen, in Boston, paintings and etchings of Johnston's. This is a description from *New England Genre* published by the Fogg Art Museum of Boston of one of his etchings: "A drunken man on a street corner leans against a post which is surmounted by a mortar, the sign of the drug store at the right. He looks at the shadow of the mortar which he has mistaken for that of his own hat. A few passersby are on the street." This might well describe a Blythe painting of a decade later. A water color of Johnston's, probably the sketch for a painting called *Militia Muster,* which was shown at the Boston Athenaeum in 1829, is full of the spirit that appears later in Blythe's genre. A grotesque horde of humanity is lined up in review. One militiaman has whacked his neighbor with the butt of his rifle; another has knocked his partner's hat off with his bayonet as he swung the gun to his shoulder; another has jabbed the man next to him in the seat of the trousers with the end of his rifle. And so it goes. Blythe must have enjoyed this! So this twist of fate which carried Blythe's ship to Boston may have contributed something to his growth as an artist, and cannot be overlooked by those who try to find the hidden pools that fed his development.

Later in January the "Ontario" went south again. It stopped at Pensacola, and on March 22 reached Vera Cruz. April 6 it sailed into Tampico, then back to Pensacola May 12. From September 24 until October 14 it was at Nassau, and was again at Pensacola October 28. The log shows that it docked at Fort Pickens on November 10, and was on January 1, 1840, at Sacrificio. Apparently it cruised this area until March 6, when it touched at Havana. It returned to Pensacola on April 1, where a dramatic incident occurred. This was the court-martialling and execution of Fleming Livingston. "The ships of the fleet gathered about the flagship 'Macedonia,'" says the log, "to witness the hanging of the offender. He stood on the scaffold with the rope about his neck when reprieve was suddenly granted, bringing the incident to a dramatic close." If Blythe made a sketch of this unusual scene, no trace of it remains.

May 13 records the ship at Havana once more, and at sea again from May 16 until May 28. Thereafter, the log, which is preserved in the Library of Congress, is incomplete. But, since Blythe's three years of service were nearly fulfilled, it is reasonable to assume that when the ship cruised northward, he was honorably discharged from the Brooklyn Navy Yard, probably in August, 1840. The log is the only record remaining of Blythe's naval career, but his admirers will have little difficulty in visualizing the lanky, red-bearded seaman, rugged, witty, rollicking, convivial, who held his own with the best of them aboard ship and on shore leave. He made friends easily, for his sense of humor was lively, and his sharp black eyes and vivid red beard made him a man to catch attention. He was fearless and independent, and deeply loyal to his friends and convictions.

The brief entries in the ship's log are interesting, for they show that Blythe saw something of a world beyond the forks of the Allegheny and that in the course of this experience, somewhere, he may have met crosscurrents of art that affected him deeply. It is strange that no definite trace of this sea experience is found in his paintings. If he painted at all during this time, there is no evidence of it. Nor do the later paintings we have take for subjects people and places he must have seen—great masted schooners, dirty little fishing boats, sailors and buccaneers and rovers of the sea, dark-skinned natives, exotic flowers and trees, land and seascapes with purple mountains, glassy bays, picturesque villages, cluttered wharves, and the clear brilliance of tropical seas and skies. All this seems to have escaped his fancy. Blythe was never a brilliant colorist. Because he was not interested in color, scenes of the tropics may have had a foreign strangeness that left no impression. We know, too, that he cared little for landscapes and painted them rarely. The West Indies apparently failed to stir him; he found nothing of the emotional and romantic appeal that LaFarge and Homer found. The murky muddy streets of Pittsburgh, instead, inspired his finest and sincerest painting.

David Blythe was in his early twenties when he left the Navy. New York lay across the river from the Navy Yard on his route home. It may have been a time for celebration or it may have been a time for exploration. Once again, as with the Boston visit, we can only speculate. Whether he spent his time at the Bowery or at the Art Union no one knows. If he visited the latter, it introduced him to important trends in American painting. The Union was showing at that time works of Mount, Bingham, Quidor, and Woodville, and perhaps, less to Blythe's liking, paintings by Cropsey, Huntington, and Vanderlyn.

According to catalogues of sales and exhibits preserved in the New York Historical Society some paintings by old masters were being displayed in New York in the early 1840's. James Bleecher and Company on the corner of Broadway and Chambers were exhibiting paintings of the Italian, Flemish, French, and English schools; and Aaron Levy and Rollins Wilkins Company, both on lower Broadway, were showing the works of European masters. Unfortunately the catalogues are not detailed enough to indicate the paintings Blythe may have seen, but it is possible that he acquired then some of the fondness for Dutch and Flemish masters that characterizes his later paintings.

There is the possibility, too, that Blythe visited the top floor gallery which Luman Reed had in his home. Reed was well known for his hospitality and his sincere interest in young American artists, no matter how obscure.

Perhaps Blythe's wanderings led him to the City Hall where a great portrait collection was already gathered. At this date, he could have seen no less than eleven Trumbulls, seven Jarvises, four Morses, two Sullys, and paintings by Inman, Catlin, Waldo, Jewett, Rembrandt Peale, Huntington, and Page. An imposing portrait seen there, of Lafayette by Morse perhaps was in Blythe's mind when he carved his statue of the general in Uniontown a few years later.

Blythe's trek homeward possibly took him through Philadelphia, for it was on the usual route to the West. Philadelphia, in spite of the impressive list of artists working there, probably offered Blythe little. The oldest art institution in the United States, the Pennsylvania Academy of Fine Arts, had only a collection of casts, a few old masters, some early American portraits, and a small group of paintings in the grand "historic" style of West. Edwin Austin Abbey, a pupil at the Academy later, says, "What a fusty, fudgy place that Pennsylvania Academy was . . . . the trail of Rembrandt Peale and of Charles Leslie, of Benjamin West and all the dismal persons who thought themselves 'Old Masters' was over the place . . . . " Yet Philadelphia was the center for the publication of art books and periodicals that featured engravings. From eastern presses rolled numbers of art books, some paper-backed, some elaborately bound, filled with illustrations, cartoons, and guides to drawing and painting. Carl W. Drepperd gives an idea of these: "Between newspaper advertisements, town and country posters and sales bills, and the religious and temperance, even the poorest amateur had something in the way of a 'swipe-file' to help him with the least part of his genre composition." He cites more than one hundred art books published in the East in the first half of the century. While no copybook artist and too independent and original to use a "swipe-file," Blythe may have looked at some of these and from them acquired suggestions of subjects and some rudiments of color theory, perspective, and composition. Though Blythe had no formal art training at an art academy and never was taught by an eminent painter, he did have the valuable schooling of travel and observation. He had seen part of the world beyond the Alleghenies—its people, its places, and its pictures.

Chapter Two

ITINERANT PORTRAITS – LAFAYETTE STATUE – MARRIAGE – THE PANORAMA LAST PORTRAITS

BLYTHE RETURNED to East Liverpool and became an itinerant portrait painter. He spent the next five years there working at the only painting for which a young artist could find much of a market. If an artist could paint quickly and make a reasonable likeness of the sitter, his pictures were in demand in those pre-camera days. East Liverpool was prosperous, thriving from its growing pottery industries. The names Knowles, Harker, Thompson, Vodrey, and Morris are identified with this early industry, and from these leaders Blythe got some portrait commissions.

In these years he painted portraits: *John Blythe,* his father; his mother, *Susan Blythe; Mrs. Cynthia Logan; William F. Morris; Isaac Watt Knowles; James Logan; Mrs. Jeremiah Webber and Son.* These bear the characteristics of the itinerant portrait painter, and could have been done by other painters, untrained and ungifted. They are primitive. Some see them as flat, a little rigid and stiff, pallid, and lacking in color and modelling. Others see in them an archaic simplicity and charm. Of their sincerity there is no question. In spite of their woodenness they reveal genuinely the sitter's character. Lloyd Goodrich says they are "honest works showing a genuine sense of character, but marked by a woodenness and meagreness typical of the provincial limner." This seems an excellent summary of their quality. They are the work of one who was an unsophisticated artist, who painted with great care and labored effort, but who never for a moment compromised his earnestness and honesty.

Ten years later Blythe returned to East Liverpool and the portraits painted at that time are interesting to compare with his first attempts at portraiture.

Sometime during the winter of 1846-1847, Blythe's wanderings took him to Uniontown, a lively little town on the old National Pike about forty miles south of Pittsburgh. He seems to have found it to his liking, for he stayed there five years. These years were important years in Blythe's life. At Uniontown he carved an eight-foot statue of General Lafayette for the dome of the Fayette County courthouse; there, too, he painted his most ambitious work, a three hundred-foot panorama, which is the center of much speculation today. At Uniontown he courted Julia Keffer, and there she died less than a year after their marriage, a tragedy that may have been one cause of his eccentric, restless living and later painting. Uniontown and the near-by town of Waynesburg inspired most of his poetry, which for all its irregularities of rhythm and rhyme, is an important clue to the understanding of Blythe's character and personality.

In Uniontown he went to board at the Seaton House, later known as the West End Hotel. Besides Blythe, other young men lived there. One was F. H. Rice, a shoe merchant, who drove about the countryside exchanging his merchandise for produce which he converted into cash in town. The story is told that during one of these trips Rice fell asleep on his wagon. His horse, unguided, wandered too near the edge of the road, upset the cart down the embankment, and tumbled out Rice and all his produce—onions, butter, eggs, apples, and a live turkey gobbler. Later, at dinner, Rice told his experience in his dry Yankee way and his fellow boarders thought it a fine joke. One Sunday morning a short time later when the men came down for breakfast, there was over the mantelpiece a sketch Blythe had labeled "Rice's Landing." There was no mistaking what was caricatured, and since Rice's Landing was the name of a town nearby on the river, the pun added to the humor of the sketch. Rice was provoked, but the others enjoyed Blythe's witty drawing. The story is of little importance except that it shows the delight in genre reappearing in Blythe's work, which prompted the sketches on the woodshed door years before, and which years later permeates the paintings of Pittsburgh life. Blythe is always at his best in genre; it seems unfortunate that *Rice's Landing* is the only example of it to come from the Uniontown period.

Opposite the Seaton House was a store kept by Peter Uriah Hook. Over this general store Blythe rented a studio which he characteristically called "Rat's Nest." There he painted portraits rather than genre scenes, probably because there was a greater market for them, and there, over the signature of "Boots," he wrote much of his poetry. His first portrait was of one Andy Gardner. Other portraits soon followed as the townspeople learned that a young artist had just opened a studio over Peter Hook's store. The Hooks, themselves, were among Blythe's first customers; he painted both Peter and his wife. The *James T. Gorley* and the *William Searight* portraits date from these first months in Uniontown. They all have the qualities of his early East Liverpool portraits. They are flat

MRS. JEREMIAH WEBBER AND SON
(A. E. Webber, East Liverpool, O.)

STATUE OF GENERAL LAFAYETTE
(Fayette County Courthouse, Uniontown, Pa.)

in modelling, meager in color, stiff in pose, severe in their simplicity. But though they lack charm, personality, and grace, they are honest, straightforward. The townspeople must have liked them very much. The story is told in Uniontown that Blythe's portraits were so lifelike that dignified old Judge Nathaniel Ewing, passing down the street one day, bowed in his most courtly manner to a Blythe portrait in a store window, and said to it, "Good morning." Years later this portrait was taken to Greensboro, Pennsylvania, to be photographed. As it stood partly hidden in the photographer's window, a woman living across the street, who knew the subject of the picture was dead, almost fainted when she saw what seemed to her the gentleman himself.

In time Blythe moved from the Seaton House to the Eagle Hotel kept by Aaron Stone. Blythe and Stone became fast friends and Blythe remained there until a brawl of some sort took place at the hotel. Although Blythe is believed to have had no part in it, he chose to leave when the other boarders were asked to find rooms elsewhere. He moved to the famed old National House, run by Joshua Marsh, on the Turnpike, and he lived there until he left Uniontown, late in 1851. While he was at Aaron Stone's he wrote a poem to Aaron's young daughter and painted a portrait of Aaron himself, in style like the other portraits of the period.

These early portraits must have brought Blythe a fair income, for he lodged at the most respectable hotels in Uniontown. And his reputation as an artist evidently was high. He was commissioned to carve a statue of Lafayette for the new Fayette County courthouse dome. The courthouse, designed by Samuel Bryan, Jr., of Harrisburg, was completed in December, 1847. It was a two-story red brick structure, 85 feet long and 58 feet wide, and was built at a cost of $16,000. It had a porticoed façade, and a dome crowning the cupola

"Whereon might stand the chaste outline of one,
Who was the friend of Washington"

wrote Blythe, in one of his many verses of this period.

Blythe set to work drawing sketches, using as a model a large woodcut of Lafayette published by S. G. Goodrich and E. Hopkins, of New York, and lent him by Nathaniel Brownfield of Uniontown. Next he selected two-inch poplar planks from the lumber shed of Colonel William B. Robertson. They had been sawed by Harrison Wiggins at his mill at Kentuck near Ohiopyle. Blythe carted these to a log house on South Street owned by Enos West and popularly called West's Schoolhouse because the building had once housed a school. Amos Joliffe helped pin the planks together with long wooden pins. From this mass Blythe fashioned, at first with only a foot adz, the contours and form, and then, slowly and painstakingly, he refined it until an eight-foot, two-inch statue of General Lafayette emerged. The finished figure is sturdy and dignified; its workmanship suits the medium. It has admirable strength, restraint, and simplicity. The high silk hat which the General holds in his hand was made of tin by Joseph Wylie. The hat still shows the rifle shots fired into it by young hoodlums many years ago.

Funds for this statue were raised in a rather ingenious way. Bryan brought to Uniontown an awkward, bandy-legged boy named John Brown, who mounted the disc on the dome and danced and performed antics that amused the crowds in the street below. A hat was passed for contributions. Besides, a subscription paper for funds was circulated by Norval H. Hellen; Peter Hook contributed the first dollar. After $125 had been raised, the contributions gradually dwindled. Blythe was greatly dissatisfied; his statue, he asserted, was worth at least double that sum.

The street was thronged the day the statue was hauled to the courthouse and hoisted into place. That morning Joshua Speer had given it a finished coat of gun-metal gray paint, for which the commissioners paid him $25. And atop the dome the statue stood, imposing and resplendent, until the building was torn down fifty years later to make way for a new courthouse. Then the statue was left to the oblivion of Alex D. Ewing's carriage house. But a later generation replaced it near its old site. It was for a time in the courthouse grounds. Today it stands in the corridor of the new courthouse. But posterity has not been content, it seems, merely to restore the statue to a place of honor; a house painter was assigned the job of repainting it. Mr. Alfred E. Jones, Jr., of Uniontown, comments on this in a letter dated April 7, 1947:

> . . . . he (the statue) now has a face, ears, and hands of an approximate flesh color, brown hair and blue eyes. His shirt is white with a green stock (necktie) and his waistcoat is a sort of rose color with brown lapels and brown buttons. He is wearing gray pants and his coat and hat are black and his walking stick is the same rose color as his waistcoat . . . he looks very gay.

The statue is gay after the fashion of cigar store Indians. The coloring has spoiled the lines and texture of the carving. It is to be hoped that the statue will be restored to its former state.

Blythe made one other carving, probably during the last few months of his stay in Uniontown. This was the *Eagle and Beehive* shop sign for the store of Lippincott and Shallenberger. The carving, about two feet high, shows an eagle with outspread wings, perched on a beehive. It is skillfully designed, with great vigor and simplicity, and is carved with real feeling for the medium. The carving was found years later in the attic of a Main Street shop, less than a block from where Lippincott and Shallenberger displayed the sign of the Golden Beehive when they opened their store in the Bryan

Building, on April 1, 1852. Today it is owned by Mr. Horace Frost of Uniontown.

The year 1847 must have been a happy one in Blythe's life. At thirty-two he was something of a success. The statue of Lafayette was the talk of the town and the surrounding country. He had a good income from his portrait painting. He had made many friends and was liked and respected. And he became engaged to Julia Keffer, who by all accounts was charming, intelligent, and beautiful. Her diary has this entry: "Made an engagement of marriage with David G. Blythe, April 5th, 1847."

Julia Keffer was the daughter of Christian Keffer, who settled in Uniontown sometime before 1830. Julia is believed to have been born in a frame house on Second Street just east of the Mansion Pottery in East Liverpool, February 28, 1824. The Keffers were the first Catholics to come to Uniontown. Once a month the Reverend Father Thomas McGowan celebrated Mass at the Keffer home at the west end of Peter Street near the Methodist Church, until St. John's Church was built at Morgantown and Center streets about 1850. Julia's brother, John, became a citizen of some prominence in Uniontown. He was associated at one time with Andrew Byers and L. W. Stockton in the dry goods business, and, later, was Register of Deeds, Recorder of Wills, and finally Clerk of Orphans Court.

Of Julia and Blythe's courtship we know almost nothing. We do know that Blythe was, at that time, gay, impetuous, and ardent. Only a few verses scribbled in an autograph album give a glimpse of their romance. Blythe often added a line or so to verses written in Julia's album. Julia's sister-in-law had written:

An album is as odd a thing as you may chance to meet,
Where everyone may drop a line of something short and sweet,

A storehouse of sweet remains, a lighthouse on life's sea
Still whispering in the ear, dear girl, remember me.

Blythe added:

It is another thing besides "lighthouse" or "store of sweets";
It is a Rock whereon the tide of boisterous memory beats.

Miss Hester Smith had written:

True friendship is a gordian knot
Which angels' hands have tied,
By heavenly skill its textures wrought
Who can its folds divide?

Blythe added:

I think you're under a mistake—
Though angels' hands have tied it,
A dollar sometimes makes it break,
So say they who have tried it.

To some verses of Ferdinand Keffer for his sister Julia, Blythe added this quatrain:

Whate'er thoughts thy sister's name
May have aroused in thee,
Are but the sparks beside the flame
It kindles up in me.

The next year, Blythe and Julia Keffer drove to Pittsburgh where, in the rectory of old St. Paul's Cathedral on Grant Street, they were married on September 30, 1848. They were of different religious faiths, and something of Blythe's devotion to Julia is suggested by his willingness to be married by a Roman Catholic priest. They returned to Uniontown and lived at the National House. But within a year, in the summer of 1849, Julia Blythe died of typhoid fever. She is buried at Brownsville, not far from Uniontown. Blythe soon after his wife's death wrote:

They told me you were dying,
And a tear, the first I'd seen
For years, flowed down my cheek,
And seemed to mollify the keen
Bitterness of departed hope.

And recollections spread her wing,
And hurrying back into the past,
Brought, one by one, each little thing
That bound us to each other. And
There clustering around, they spoke
Something to me, in thy name,
And my heart was broke.

'Tis past! The door is shut and locked
And darkness, darker grown
With being mocked
By light and hope, has shown
Me, I'm alone!

'Tis past! And all again is blank.
The little bark that bore me on
Its wing is sunk;
And every spark of hope is gone,
And I'm alone.

'Tis past! And now my wandering eye
Dim by disappointment grown,
Meets but the sky
As dark and starless as its own—
For I'm alone.

'Tis past! There was but one unbroken link
That held me trembling on the brink;
But that is gone,
And now I sink!
Alone! Alone!

The verses may be jagged and unsure as poetry, and often phrased conventionally but they suggest sincerely if roughly a deep and intimate devotion.

The records of Julia Blythe are so few that, at best, only dim conjectures can be made of the effect on Blythe of her life and death. It is commonly held that Blythe was deeply affected by her death. A friend wrote: "After her death the beauty and the worth seemed to have departed out of his life." The Uniontown historian, James Hadden, says, "A gloominess, caused by the loss of his bosom companion, settled over the life of Blythe, from which he never fully recovered. He became extremely careless of his dress and utterly regardless of the opinions of his fellow man." This last we know to be true. Once he cut a piece from a buffalo robe and sewed it together as a hat. It covered his head and most of his face; his friends recognized him only by his tall angular frame and long, swinging strides. To go with his hat, he made himself a suit. He sat, Turk fashion, on the floor of Ab Guiler's Tailor Shop, and without a pattern cut out a suit and sewed it together himself. Although Ab told him it "hung on him like a bean pole" he wore it for some time, ignoring all criticism. Because we know that Blythe was passionate and emotional, it is easy to believe that often he felt his grief and loneliness to be more than he could bear and that he expressed his sorrow in strange ways. On the other hand, Blythe was a vigorous, energetic person who loved people and action. It seems likely, therefore, that generally he was able to throw off his despair and continue his interests and activities, and that he painted, and met with his friends as before.

Not long after Julia's death Blythe was asked by a committee of Greene County officials to carve a statue of General Nathaniel Greene for the dome of a new courthouse to be built by Samuel Bryan, Jr. at Waynesburg, twenty or so miles from Uniontown. Blythe, elated by praise of his Lafayette statue, asked $300 for the statue of General Greene. The committee was outraged. They stalked home declaring that "they did not propose to give him the whole county for his work and in all probability they had local artists who could do as well for one hundred dollars." And they promptly hired a local wood carver, Bradley Mahanna. Blythe, with a temper as fiery as his red hair, was infuriated. He turned to verse to express his feelings for Greene County in general and Waynesburg in particular, referring on one occasion to the former as "a sow grown fat with buttermilk and meal." For more than a year the rhymes appeared in the *Uniontown Democrat,* edited by Jacob B. Miller, and in the *American Standard,* edited by John F. Beazell. Occasionally they were answered by Waynesburg's poet, William Siegfried, whom Blythe called "a pumpkin-headed poet" and for a time verbal blows were exchanged, much to the delight of the people of Greene and Fayette counties. Blythe declared:

> Waynesburg is built upon a hill,
> Where everything you chance to spill runs off.
> A pious notion, bye the bye—
> All finished things should occupy
> A situation high and dry,
>   for fear of spoil.

For more than one hundred lines Blythe continued to satirize Waynesburg. When the cornerstone for the new courthouse was laid in June, 1850, Blythe followed up those taunts with another long poem in the same spirit.

Just before his marriage, Blythe became interested in Masonic activities, and after Julia's death he seems to have given much time to Masonic affairs. On the evening of May 9, 1848, Blythe was initiated into Fayette Lodge No. 228 of Free Masons. He passed to the degree of Fellowcraft on April 6, 1850, and was raised to Master Mason May 18, 1850. At a meeting of the Lodge on August 12, 1850, Colonel T. B. Searight proposed that Brother Blythe be commissioned to paint a portrait for the lodge hall of Brother John W. Irons, Worshipful Master of the Lodge, who had died the month before. This motion, referred to a committee, was reported on favorably, and Blythe painted the portrait for $16. From the wall of the lodge hall, young Mr. Irons looks down today, dignified and resplendent in his Masonic collar; but the painting is faded by time and marred by bad cleaning, and is flat in modelling and lifeless in color.

When the cornerstone of the Waynesburg courthouse was laid with Masonic ceremonies on June 25, 1850, Blythe and several brother Masons were there to help celebrate. Out of his experiences at the Bull's Head Hotel, where he and his friends stayed, Blythe wrote some more doggerel published on January 1, 1851, in the *Pennsylvania Democrat* and the *Greene County Whig*. Here are a few of its one hundred lines:

Greene county had a holiday
And Waynesburg never looked so gay
As when the Masons went to lay
That corner stone.

And, by the by, here let me say,
Tho' some may deem it flattery,
That such of prejudice that day
And mist and fog have swept away
From eyes and heart and heads grown gray
In ignorance of Masonry in old Greene.

It was the tallest day, I ween,
The b'hoys up there had ever seen
Since she became the "state of Greene"
Mr. Speaker.

There was a motley gathering there—
Red-hot from almost everywhere—
Prepared like Tam O'Shanter's mare,
To see fun before they got home.

Blythe found some time to paint a few portraits, which cannot be found. Among these are the *William A. West, Mrs. William A. West,* and *John Kimberly*. One of John Keffer, Blythe's brother-in-law, was destroyed in a fire many years ago. These probably were painted either as gestures of friendship or for the small sums that they brought him; Blythe's heart was not in them. He was nursing an idea planted in the days of his trip down the Mississippi with his brother John. By 1850 the fame of the panoramists had spread far and wide. Tales of the fabulous fortunes being made by these painters undoubtedly reached Uniontown. Henry Lewis had finished a panorama 12 feet high and 1,325 yards long, glorifying the Father of Waters, and had shown it in Cincinnati in the summer of 1849. As early as 1847 another panorama, John Banvard's "three miles of canvas," was exhibited in Louisville, and later moved to Boston and New York; ultimately it was taken to London where it "dazzled 600,000 Englishmen when displayed at Windsor Castle." In 1848 John Rowson Smith entertained American spectators with a canvas "four miles long," which he, too, took to Europe and showed with very profitable results. When Blythe heard these things, he dreamed of fame and money which his portraits could never yield him. With characteristic vigor, he decided that he, too, would paint a panorama. He planned that his panorama would show historical events and natural scenery from Albemarle County, Virginia, up through the Ligonier Valley of Pennsylvania. So he spent months making sketches in the valleys of Maryland, Virginia, and Pennsylvania. On one of these trips, Tom Campbell, a clerk in Dr. Hugh Campbell's "Medicine Store," went with Blythe. They made their headquarters at Harden's Hotel in Bradonville, Pennsylvania. Another time his companion was Hugh Gorley. Gorley tells of holding the horse while Blythe made one of his sketches. It seemed to him to be an immense spider just out of a bath in a pool of ink and stepping out on the paper to plume itself.

In February, 1850, Blythe planned another sketching jaunt, this time with James T. Gorley. He expected to be gone a fairly long time. Before he went he wrote these lines in the "Rat's Nest," February 27, 1850:

> Farewell awhile, sweet Uniontown,
>   The cords are snapping one by one,
> The wheels will soon be rolling round
>   And "Boots" be with his follies gone.

For a number of lines he bids farewell to his friends, addressing them by name–Hankins (Peter Hook), George (Hubbs), Barge (Shallenberger), Ab (Guiler), Norve (Hellen), and so on. He concludes:

> When absent, dreams will bring me back
>   In pleasure or perhaps in pain
> Imagination's lip may smack
>   And goblets drank, be drunk again.
>
> To every friend, to every foe,
>   To every frown, to every smile,
> To who says yes, to who says no,
>   To each, to all, farewell awhile.

In the end "Skinner" (James T. Gorley) could not go with him. Blythe set out alone in March and made many sketches. Back again in Uniontown, he began the great panorama. January 1, 1851, Blythe, James T. Gorley, and Peter U. Hook entered into an agreement that Gorley and Hook would furnish the money and Blythe would do the painting. Because it was larger than the "Rat's Nest," Blythe rented as a studio the upper room of No. 7 East Main Street, which later was the tailor shop of T. W. Bulger.

There Blythe lost himself in his dream. He was not often on the streets those days or at the lodge hall. He let only his most intimate friends watch, in the cluttered studio, the large sections take form.

Each scene was painted on a 7′ × 15′ section, and these were sewed together into a continuous strip. The finished strip had twenty sections; it was 300 feet long. Slowly, like a massive scroll wound on revolving cylinders, it was to be revealed to spectators who paid admission to see its unfolding. Although Blythe's panorama was small compared to Banvard's and some others, the amount of effort put into the work is impressive.

The panorama has long been disassembled and undoubtedly destroyed. It is impossible to discuss it in detail. Nothing is known of its technical merits. What its color range was we can only imagine in the light of Blythe's later work, but perhaps even such speculation is unfair because he never again tried this sort of painting. We do know from brief descriptions of a few of the scenes that the scenery painted is some of the most magnificent in America; it is regrettable that we know so little of his interpretation and representation of it. One section showed lovely Monticello, with Charlottesville in the distance. Another showed the Potomac winding through the rocky gap at Harper's Ferry; another showed the Natural Bridge. It is said there were other scenes along the Potomac and along the route that Washington followed from Cumberland in his expedition against the French in 1754. Washington's army at Fort Necessity was the subject of another scene, and so were the encampments of Braddock's army, the burial of Braddock, Big Rocks where Jumonville was killed and buried, and Washington and Christopher Gist in consultation. In other sections were Washington Springs, the encampment of Colonel Dunbar; Arthur St. Clair sitting in front of his log tavern with the Ligonier Valley stretching beyond; Jacob B. Miller fishing at Ohiopyle Falls; Uniontown from Pine Knob; White Rocks where Polly Williams was murdered by her lover in 1810. What other scenes there were, we do not know.

When the last dab of paint had been applied and the last section joined, the three sets of rollers on which the canvas was mounted were loaded into the stagecoach. When all was ready, Gorley mounted to the driver's seat. At the last moment Louis D. Beall rushed out from the crowd gathered to see the departure, and offered Gorley $1,000 for his interest in the panorama, but Gorley was enthusiastic enough to refuse the offer. So with a rattle, the tour moved off to the accompanying shouts and well wishes of the crowd.

They drove through the mountains to little Cumberland, sixty miles to the east. On October 3, 1851, they began a seven-day exhibition. Lin Hunt and Nels Patrick explained each scene with appropriate oratory as the scroll was unwound; Blythe, Hook, and Gorley managed the unwinding. At the close of the week they went south to Winchester, where the familiar and historic settings and events delighted the Virginians, and then east to Baltimore where they rented a hall for $40 a week. In Baltimore the panorama was enthusiastically received. The three owners and their assistants were jubilant.

Pittsburgh was their next stop. Blythe was eager to exhibit his masterpiece to old friends. Philo Hall on Third Street, the home of the Philological Society, was rented, and on the ninth of December it was crowded for the showing of the panorama. Ironically enough, it was at Pittsburgh that the first shadow of coming failure fell. Blythe could not resist delivering the accompanying lecture, and apparently made so bungling a failure of it that the evening was far less successful than others had been. Soon after, Hook, who had been elected to the legislature at the election of October 15, 1851, withdrew. He offered to sell his interest. This action broke the spirit of the enterprise, for Hook had been its dominant figure. The panorama was stored temporarily in Philo Hall while a reorganization was undertaken.

Finally, Blythe's old friend, Norval H. Hellen, took hold of the matter. He and Blythe started down the Ohio with the panorama. They exhibited the work at Blythe's hometown, East Liverpool, and again the audience was enthusiastic. Encouraged, they pushed on to Cincinnati, but for some unknown reason Hellen withdrew, and Blythe was left stranded. The panorama was held for freight. E. N. Fowler, a tinner in Uniontown, saw the Cincinnati advertisement, and notified Hook and Gorley. They raised the $115 needed, redeemed the panorama, and carted it back to Uniontown. There Hook put it in condition again in the back room of his store. It is not known that Blythe had a part in this work.

The panorama was next shown in the new Fremont Hall, on the corner of Main and Morgantown streets, with John L. Means explaining the scenes. The audience was a large one, and hilarious, and they turned out with a will to see Dave Blythe's panorama they had been hearing about so many months. A story is handed down from that time. In one picture, a stag with immense horns is shown emerging from a dense forest. One of the audience stood up and asked, "How does that deer get through the thicket with those big horns?" The squire was disconcerted. He stopped. Pointing a bony finger at the questioner, he snapped, "That's his business."

In another scene Blythe had painted fowls and farmyard creatures. Hugh Gorley had concealed a tank of water which the audience could not see, and had borrowed some white ducks from Norval Greenland and set them in the tank. The spectators then saw an incredible phenomenon: the ducks began to swim about and dive for bits of corn. This realistic touch almost brought on a riot as, amazed, the crowd tried to swarm to the platform to find how Dave Blythe had managed to paint ducks so real they dived and swam. It took the most strenuous efforts of the management to keep their secret and restore order in the hall. In the next day's newspaper, the town poet wrote:

While some believe that Blythe could paint
A portrait that could speak,
They ne'er conceived that he could paint
A little duck that eat.

After this spectacular showing, Daniel Shupe appeared in the somewhat complicated business, somehow acquired the panorama, and took it to Mt. Pleasant, where he displayed it for a time. Then he stored it in his distillery. We have no record that Blythe went to Mt. Pleasant. His only connection with Mt. Pleasant so far as is known is through his genre painting, *The Woodchopper*, which, until recently, was owned by the Fleming family of that community. It is quite possible that Blythe went to Mt. Pleasant with the panorama and at that time painted *The Woodchopper*.

A Doctor Kelly from that region had helped Shupe buy out Hook's interest for $300 and he traveled west with the panorama, reportedly making some money. He came back with it to Mt. Pleasant on April 18, 1852, and sold his interest to a man named Bear, who tried to buy the share still held by Gorley. But Gorley wanted cash, and the sale fell through. After this the wanderings and business transactions of the panorama became very complex. Norval Hellen, still believing that the project could make money if properly managed, offered for it all his stock of dry goods, groceries, and queensware valued at between $2,500 and $3,000. Gorley would not sell. Bear then divided the canvas in half and took his section on a tour through Ohio. Gorley retrieved his half, which still was stored in Shupe's distillery, brought it to Uniontown, and set it up in his store.

Sometime later, when Gorley was in Pittsburgh, he met sculptor Isaac Broome. In their talk the panorama was mentioned. Broome offered to buy the canvas and went to Uniontown with Gorley, where the sale was completed. Gorley's half of the panorama then left Uniontown for the last time. Broome was eager to secure the other half but his efforts to locate it were unsuccessful. It may have gone the way that Broome's half went; his was never displayed and is believed to have been cut in pieces and sold to Trimble's Variety Show for backdrops.

Blythe's part in these later transactions is not clear. He seems to have been ignored after the Cincinnati debacle. Probably he never made any money from the project, but, perhaps even more disheartening to him, was its ignominious ending. To know that it was cut in pieces and scattered about western Pennsylvania, some of it serving as backdrops in a theatre, was probably more of a blow to his pride than the disappointment in not realizing the fortunes of Bierstadt and Banvard.

One matter may well be speculated upon before leaving this period of Blythe's career. His stay in Cincinnati during the tour may have given him a chance to see the work of artists living and painting there. It is possible that the harrassed Blythe spent all his time trying to get his panorama and himself out of town, for it is reported that he was "flat broke." Yet, on the other hand, he was insatiably curious. He loved wandering about streets, and he may have caught something of the culture that Cincinnati of the 1850's had to offer. By this

THOMAS COBURN
(Mary G. Irwin, East Liverpool, O.)

ART VERSUS LAW
(Brooklyn Museum)

time Cincinnati had established itself among the western cities as a leader in art. The Beard brothers were painting animals—comic and moralizing beasts—of great popularity. William H. Powell, a student of Inman, was an outstanding painter of great historical pictures, one of which was placed in the rotunda of the Capitol in Washington. The literary-inspired paintings of Thomas Buchanan Read were popular. The Hudson River School landscapes of William Sonntag frequently were exhibited. Cincinnati had an Academy of Fine Arts, of which Godfrey H. Frankenstein was the first president, and, in 1847, the Western Art Union, patterned after the American Art Union in New York, was established. Cole's "Voyage of Life" and the work of Worthington Whittredge and J. O. Eaton were exhibited there. Although Cincinnati's greatest artists appeared a little later, definite artistic forces were alive in the city when Blythe was there. He may have met some of them.

It becomes more and more obvious that the interpretation of Blythe as a backwoods artist has been overemphasized. A man of his keen powers of observation and mental agility undoubtedly absorbed much from his visits to cities where art was thriving. By his thirty-fifth year he had seen the Mississippi Valley, New Orleans, St. Louis, New York, Boston, Atlantic seaports, the West Indies, and probably Philadelphia. All of these must be considered as contributing, directly and indirectly, in the development not only of Blythe the man but of Blythe the artist. Whether these factors were primary ingredients or mere seasoning in his career is difficult to say, but any study of Blythe and his painting must take them into consideration.

David Blythe left Uniontown late in 1851. So far as we know he returned only once, on an excursion train to a political gathering in the fall of 1864. He is said to have shaken hands hurriedly with a few old friends, and then to have left as soon as he could. This may be true. It is understandable. Uniontown held memories of sorrow and disappointment. We know that Blythe was emotional, at times sentimental, and it is quite possible that he never fully recovered from Julia's death and the failure of the panorama. Unquestionably, when he quietly left Uniontown in 1851 he was a very discouraged young man. But the Blythe who wandered rather aimlessly away was far more mature than the Blythe who strode down Uniontown's narrow streets six years before, to build a reputation as an artist. He had lost much of the lightheartedness he had when he was courting Julia; when he left he wore a "suit" which "hung on him like a bean-pole." He had lost, too, the high hopes and driving ambitions with which he set about carving the statue and painting the panorama. But in their place, if we are to judge him by his paintings, had come a deeper understanding of life and people. His sorrow and disappointment had not hardened him and made him bitter and cynical; instead, they seem to have sharpened his insight into life, wakened tolerance for the weakness and failure in others. In 1851, it seems, Blythe's chance of much success as an artist was at its lowest. His portraits so far were no more distinguished than those of scores of itinerant portraitists. And his most ambitious painting, the panorama, hung in bits as a stage backdrop! Yet he was on the threshold of his finest work. The blows to his pride and happiness that fell at Uniontown seem to have made him more sensitive. So he was able to bring into his painting sympathy and warmth that kept his humor gentle and never sharp, his satire mild and never bitter.

Blythe's deepened maturity is shown first in the portraits that he painted in East Liverpool the next few years. These portraits of the early 1850's are the best—and the last—that he painted. They mark the highest level of his portrait painting; in Pittsburgh, the last decade of his life, he painted only genre and Civil War subjects.

Among these last portraits, still in East Liverpool, are the *Thomas Coburn, Mrs. Thomas Coburn, George S. Harker, Esq.*, and *Rebecca Mary Patterson,* all painted in 1853 and 1854. They have vital color; the features are subtly modelled; the composition is sound; and the drawing, skillful. They are sensitive, restrained, mature. The artist who painted them understood the personality and character of his subject and the power and limitations of his medium.

Blythe shows something of the same sure, clear-cut technique in the portraits of *John Fisher* and *Mrs. John Fisher.* The two Rigby portraits, *Job Rigby* and *Eliza Rigby,* his wife, are in the same style, and polished and sophisticated far beyond the East Liverpool portraits of the 1840's. The explanation of Blythe's growth as a portrait painter is partly in his having seen in the East the work of Sully, Harding, and other painters of that quality, and partly in his deepened understanding of people.

In the 1850 period he painted several portraits of children. These, too, have the qualities of his finer portraits. There is no hint of idealization. These children are not cherubs, nor are they the ragamuffins of Blythe's later Pittsburgh paintings. The earliest of these portraits is *Fanny.* The child, dressed in pink, a color Blythe often used for children's dresses, is seated, looking seriously out from the canvas and holding a rose in her hand. The portrait, *John C. Thompson,* a year later, in 1855, shows a seated boy, in a pink dress like Fanny's. The serious face is framed with straight, blond hair, and one hand clutches a large straw hat at his side. A descendant of the subject says that the hat was originally a hoop, but when the father of the boy objected, Blythe changed it to a hat. The *Eliza Gardner* portrait shows more animation. The pose is less stiff, the expression less sober. The child, fair-haired, again dressed in pink, is playing on the floor. In one hand she holds a little toy, probably a nineteenth century type of rattle. At her side, snuggled against her, sits a black and white terrier. An interesting note of color and pattern is the rug, meticulously painted in a blue and pink allover design, reminiscent of the rugs in eighteenth century portraits.

The portrait of *Sarah Ann Rigby* recalls the *John C. Thompson* portrait. The child, her brown hair parted severely in the middle, is seated, clasping to her a straw hat trimmed with red ribbons and deep red roses. Her face is painted with sensitive care and is without the oversweet sentimentality found in so many child portraits of the time. Unfortunately, the *Tommy Blythe* portrait of Blythe's brother has been spoiled by cleaning. Only the golden curls and the red dress suggest the original color.

A little less distinguished than these topflight portraits are the *Dr. John Coburn, Mrs. John Coburn,* and *John Thompson.* Much like these in style, color, and composition are the *Charles B. Ogden, Mrs. Bawdrey, Joseph Croxall, Mrs. Gardner, Mrs. William Thompson, Josiah Thompson,* and *David Clark Thompson.* Of this type, too, are the portraits of the MacDonald family of Hookstown, Pennsylvania, recently acquired by the Butler Art Institute of Youngstown, Ohio. They all have something, however, of the warmth, color, and modelling of the best portraits of 1854 and 1855.

During these years Blythe painted four portraits in Monongahela City—*Samuel Black Bentley, Ross Bentley, Elizabeth Black,* and *Annetta Bentley.* The last is of a child and is very much like *Eliza Gardner.* Annetta is seated gracefully on the floor beside a straw hat trimmed with red and pink flowers. She holds tight on her lap a fierce little gray mongrel, who glowers at the observer. The child is delightful. Her big eyes are friendly and suggest laughter; her mouth seems ready to break into a smile. Blythe has caught the child's personality and her passing mood.

These portraits are almost the only record we have of Blythe from 1852 until he came to Pittsburgh sometime in 1856. Probably he made East Liverpool his headquarters, for many of his portraits were painted there and are still owned by East Liverpool families. However, he must have wandered through adjoining communities for we know he painted some portraits in other places. Undoubtedly many of his portraits no longer exist or are buried in attics and cellars.

If Blythe made his home chiefly in East Liverpool, as seems likely, during these itinerant portrait painting days, he found the farm very different from the farm he had known as a boy. In 1852 his father died at age seventy-four. His mother, however, lived on until 1874, dying in her ninety-first year. Both parents were buried in the Calcutta cemetery at Calcutta, Ohio. Andrew, of the six sons, seems to have been most interested in running the farm; he did so until his death in 1880. John was a steamboat captain on the Mississippi and lost his life in an accident on the river. James went west and settled in Rock Island, Illinois.

Blythe, himself, apparently did not stay entirely in East Liverpool and the community about it. A letter written by a Major A. B. Gardner shows that Blythe spent nearly a year in Indiana. The incident is of significance only in suggesting that paintings may come to light in Indiana. The major writes:

In 1853, I was travelling through the state of Indiana selling a patent right, and on registering at the Kirkner House (a hostelry still in existence) at Madison, I was informed that Dave Blythe was one of the regular boarders for nearly a year. The scourge cholera was then raging in this and neighboring towns. The barrels were being burned in the streets, business was suspended and the dead were being hauled out for burial. I was invited and assigned to Blythe's room in which were three beds, one occupied by Blythe, one by a Mr. Byerly of Greensburg, Pennsylvania (the capital of Westmoreland County), and I occupied the other. In the night Byerly complained of being very sick, but as we all had taken ample doses of "preventative" before retiring and had another bottle of "preventative" by our bedsides, we paid no attention to the complaint of the sick man and he soon became quiet. Early next morning, I arose to take some "preventative" and called the other two occupants of the room. Dave soon sprang from bed, and believing that a half pint of "preventative" was better than a gallon of water, he went to awaken Byerly and found him dead and stiff. There were seven victims carried out of that one hotel on the morning of this occurrence. I soon left for home and never heard of Blythe afterward.

Blythe himself says that he spent some time in Indiana. In a letter to Hugh Gorley in 1857, he writes, "I once visited Jesse Bright's state of Indiana." Probably widely scattered and forgotten portraits still are in Indiana.

Chapter Three

PITTSBURGH OF THE 1850's—CULTURAL LIFE NEW BUILDINGS—EXPANDING INDUSTRIES GROWTH IN POPULATION—GILLESPIE'S BLYTHE'S STUDIOS

In 1856, David Blythe came back to Pittsburgh. He came, finally and for the rest of his life, to a community he seems to have liked and one whose life and spirit aroused him to paint his best pictures—the genre paintings of its places and people. In a way, it was coming home. For Blythe, Pittsburgh was full of memories; on at least three important occasions in his life he had come to the city at the Point. He had come first, a boy of eighteen, to learn a trade; a little later, with great happiness, he had brought Julia Keffer to Pittsburgh, to marry her at Old Saint Paul's; two years after, with enthusiasm and pride, he had come to show off his panorama to old friends. But when he came back in 1856 to what were the last nine years of his life, he was neither ambitious nor happy nor proud. The great happiness of his married life had passed; his great pride in his panorama was gone. Yet, though he may have felt he was a failure, he actually was about to begin his best work. The death of his wife and the unhappy outcome of his panorama project may have taken away what little interest he ever had in money and position; yet it was lack of this interest that allowed him to paint as he did. To be sure, it may have lessened the force that could have driven him to greater work, but indifference to the commercial side of painting left him free to paint from his heart—to paint what and when he chose. He could be himself; he need not please art patron or critic. He need not bother to conform to the tastes of society, not being concerned about its money or its praise. Failure and disappointment may have sent him to the corner tavern where he wasted hours he might have spent painting, but they did not embitter him nor make him retreat into himself. Failure and disappointment may even have increased his interest in others and deepened his understanding of their sorrows and follies. At any rate, Pittsburgh in the late 1850's and early 1860's brought David Blythe into his own. Although Blythe lived and worked in Pittsburgh only nine years—he died there at fifty on May 15, 1865—he recorded with amazing insight the men and women of Pittsburgh and the backgrounds of their lives. And although during these nine years he was away from Pittsburgh at times, sometimes visiting his family in East Liverpool and once for several months following along with the Thirteenth Pennsylvania Regiment just after the outbreak of the Civil War, he caught in his paintings the spirit of the city and its customs and manners.

Blythe is something of an enigma as a man and an artist. Of his life few records exist; there are many months that we cannot account for, many times when we do not know where he lived and what he did. As a painter, he is even more of a mystery. Because he was self-taught, it is difficult to trace the development of his style. Much that he learned he picked up in his travels and in paintings he saw; it is almost impossible to find clear-cut lines of influence. His work is undoubtedly touched by many influences, some important, some insignificant. At best, one can only speculate about these and attempt to find the more important elements which affected his work. He was a painter of genre by talent and by temperament. It was in him; it came from him as naturally and instinctively in his studio in Pittsburgh as it had on the farm in East Liverpool when he was a boy. Yet there were probably two influences which, more than any others, helped to stimulate his natural desire and develop his ability to paint genre. One was the great interest in genre among American painters of that time; Blythe knew their work and the work of the European masters of genre, probably through reproductions, since he had almost no chance to study originals. The other was Pittsburgh itself, a city whose life and spirit aroused him to interpret and represent it.

The effect of the first of these two influences on Blythe's work is especially difficult to analyze and measure. Many Americans were studying abroad, at Dusseldorf and Munich, where narrative and genre art was the vogue. They came back to America and painted in this genre style. And though Blythe probably never met any of these painters, probably saw few of their paintings, he undoubtedly saw reproductions of their work. The Art Union in New York, for example, circulated prints of Bingham, Mount, and Woodville paintings. It seems likely that Blythe felt the growing interest in genre, and that, because it suited his talent and temperament and because he saw subjects and techniques that pleased him, painted it enthusiastically.

Blythe did not need to study at Dusseldorf, Munich, or Paris, or at New York, Boston, or Philadelphia to see and understand this sort of painting. It reached him in Pittsburgh, and he needed only to look about him to find subjects perfectly suited to its style and techniques. The introduction of commercial lithography in 1822 gave artists a cheap and fluent method of illustration. The result was a flood of drawings, cartoons, and caricatures. Comic almanacs were sold everywhere. *Puck, Judge,* and *The Wasp* brought caricatures into American homes. Peterson's *Illustrated Edition of Humorous Works* featured the work of Darley from 1845 on, and set a pattern which many magazines followed. Periodicals like *The Lantern* publicized the sketches of Bellew, Gunn, Stephens, and others. *Vanity Fair* flared briefly and brightly, filled with the work of Mullen and Fisk. Pittsburgh newspapers carried many advertisements by S. Sadler of Allegheny and Pittock of Fifth Street of *Harper's Magazine* and *Frank L. Leslie's Illustrated News Weekly.* These magazines were illustrated by such artists as William John Hennessy, Winslow Homer, Alfred Fredericks, Augustus Hoppin, and Thomas Nast. *Harper's* carried a page or two from *Punch,* and so gave Americans the drawings of England's John Leech, Charles Bennett, and Charles Keene.

This was a time of engravings. In the census of 1850, 2,208 American artists listed themselves as engravers. Few homes were without this inexpensive short cut to decoration. Many magazines featured engravings, chief among them the *Columbian Magazine, Godey's Lady's Book,* and *Graham's Magazine,* which had a circulation of 40,000 and needed four steel plates of each subject to serve the demand. H. S. Sadd, C. H. Bodmer, A. L. Dick, and Rawdon Wright pictured Indians, battlefields, and western scenic subjects; and W. E. Tucker was sent abroad to engrave Old Masters. By 1870 Godey's alone had published 1,000 steel plates of the work of Sartain, Croome, Dallas, Frost, and Darley. Annuals such as *Atlantic Souvenier, Token, The Hyacinth, The Gift,* and a score like them, featured the engravings of Durand, Andrews,

Smillie, and others after paintings by Allston, Coe, Leslie, and Brown. The illustrations of Darley in the novels of Poe, Irving, and Dickens were well known. Clearly, the genre style of Dusseldorf and the narrative style of Munich, adopted by countless artists, were spread over America through the media of the individual engraving, the periodical, and the novel. Blythe could not help feeling the effects of this taste and catching something of current ideas and styles. The importance of this as an influence on Blythe's art must not be overlooked.

The part which prints of all kinds, engravings, facsimiles, illustrations, reproductions, and restrikes of European masters, played in shaping taste and style and in furnishing subjects for many a self-taught American artist cannot be overemphasized in trying to find the "why" of Blythe's art. They were a rich and powerful means for spreading techniques and ideas. A painter like Blythe, denied formal training and wide opportunity to study firsthand the work of the Old Masters as well as those of his contemporaries in America and abroad, found in them inspiration and direction.

Prints of the European masters had been available in America from the eighteenth century. The painter, John Smibert, in May, 1735, advertised for sale a collection of valuable prints engraved after the paintings of Raphael, Michelangelo, Poussin, and Rubens. Early in the nineteenth century G. Milksham Brown of 359 Broadway advertised French and British prints. A catalogue of Merwin, Bangs and Company featured etchings of Ostade. J. S. Phillips of Philadelphia acquired some sixty thousand prints between 1820 and 1866, and other extensive print collections became the hobbies of men like James L. Claghorn, Henry F. Sewall, George Perkins Marsh, Robert Hoe, and Theodore Irwin who specialized in Old Masters.

Blythe's friend, J. J. Gillespie, traveled abroad in the 1850's and brought back prints of the Old Masters, which Blythe undoubtedly saw. Prints of Goya's *Los Caprichos* reached the United States. And Daumier's great caricatures were seen in the same way. There are suggestions of Daumier in Blythe, and it was only through prints that Blythe knew the great Frenchman's work. The *Pittsburgh Gazette* of January 19, 1853, advertised *The Illustrated Magazine of Art,* a monthly publication containing sixty large octave pages of foreign prints, priced at $8.00 a year.

The English caricaturist, Rowlandson, was known through his illustrations of *Dr. Syntax, The Dance of Life,* and *The Dance of Death.* Cruikshank illustrated *Oliver Twist* and the works of Smolett, Goldsmith, Fielding, and Cervantes. Americans saw the brilliant Phiz (Hablot Knight Browne) in *Pickwick Papers, Barnaby Ridge,* and *The Tale of Two Cities.* John Leech was known through *Ups and Downs of Life,* Dicken's *Christmas Carol,* and *Punch.* Gustave Doré illustrated Rabelais' *Pantagruel and Gargantua,* Balzac's *Droll Stories,* and Cervante's *Don Quixote.* The lanky, elegant knight painted by Blythe in a recently discovered painting is very like Doré's version; it suggests that Blythe saw Doré's work.

That all this European art was available to Americans through reproductions makes it reasonable to assume that characteristics in Blythe's work suggesting Ostade, Hogarth, Daumier, and others, were picked up by him in this way. This assumption seems a logical answer to why much in Blythe resembles Dutch and Flemish paintings, even though he may have seen few if any originals.

But of far greater importance than Blythe's familiarity with foreign prints and paintings was the direct influence on his art of the community in which he lived and worked. Pittsburgh of the 1850's and 1860's was a colorful, cosmopolitan, turbulent place, and Blythe was by nature interested in people, and his experience made him a sensitive interpreter of such living. The narrow, hilly, gaslighted streets and alleys channeled their ways through a maze of shops, warehouses, taverns, markets, and mansions, always crowded with crinoline-skirted ladies, busy merchants, rough rivermen, and ragged tramps. In Pittsburgh of the mid-nineteenth century, East met West, the fringe of eastern culture overlapping the fringe of western swashbucklery. The city held the spirit of the ribald, boisterous trader, the pioneer, and the river crewman; it held, too, the spirit of staid, strait-laced Presbyterian morality. It was the city of "Rowdy Joe" Barker and prim Jane Swisshelm; it was Blythe's *Pittsburgh Piety* and *Molly Maguire, Dry Goods and Notions,* and *The Hideout.*

Genre art rests upon bourgeois taste. And in America as in the Holland of the seventeenth century, this force was abroad in the land. It had its parallel in literature, too, which saw writers turning from the people of other lands and ages to tell, instead, the America they really knew. Not to be ignored, of course, were eclectic and revivalist tendencies in some of the arts, and the taste among the *nouveau riche* and the ultra-sophisticates for things European. But the opening up of the West had made the nation aware of its amazing size and resources. The result was an outburst of nationalism. Out of this democratic, bourgeois, nationalistic mid-nineteenth century, so strongly alive in the community at the forks of the Ohio, came an art close in spirit to its great predecessor in Holland two centuries before. And David Blythe emerged on its horizon, saturated with it from the top of his battered hat to the toes of his scuffed boots.

Let us follow Blythe as he tramped the narrow streets of Pittsburgh, observe what Blythe observed, and try to understand the tastes and customs and life around him that helped mold him as an artist and as a man during his golden years.

Blythe found that Pittsburgh still liked panoramas. A panorama of *Pilgrim's Progress* had been shown in Philo Hall a few years before, in 1852. *The Gazette* of November 22 pronounced it "superior to all panoramas." Only a few months before Blythe came, a panorama showing Monmouth Cave, Niagara Falls, and the Crystal Palace had been combined with a concert at the Athenaeum in a gala entertainment, "attended," reported *The Gazette,* "by an intelligent and fashionable audience."

The Pittsburgh Academy for Instruction and Painting had been organized in 1855. Its significance does not seem great, and Blythe probably paid it only a casual glance. Of greater interest to Blythe, perhaps, was a new lithography shop established about the same time by William Schuchman at Third and Market streets, where prints were exhibited from time to time.

Old Drury still stood on Fifth Street, flanked by the popular Falstaff House, where Blythe often went, and by Davis' Drugstore. At Old Drury *Uncle Tom's Cabin* had electrified audiences a year or two earlier and there John Drew and Edwin Booth played to enthusiastic crowds. So great had become the taste for the stage that the National Theatre, designed to seat 1,600, was in the process of alteration to meet the demands of Pittsburgh theater goers. Ben Trimble's *Varieties* also drew huge crowds, especially from among the red-shirted raftmen. Perhaps at the *Varieties* Blythe saw parts of his own panorama used as backdrops.

Western University of Pennsylvania was opening to the young men of the community at its new location on the southwest corner of Diamond and Ross, the present site of the City-County Building. Not far away towered the new First Presbyterian Church, finished in 1853—imposing Gothic in gray stone. Its elegant interior Blythe used, probably, in a painting recently discovered, *Pittsburgh Piety.*

The skies aglow from the coke ovens at the base of Coal Hill outlined the skeleton of the new Clinton Iron Furnace. It was being built on the south side of the Monongahela, halfway between Smithfield Street and the Point Bridge. And ground was being broken for the Eliza Furnace of Jones & Laughlin on the north bank of the river near Second Avenue. Sparks and smoke filled the air from puddling furnaces and the open-hearth furnaces and the crucible furnaces along the rivers' edges. The clang and clatter were loud from foundries along the "bottoms." "Timber Wheels" lumbered over the roads bearing huge pipes, bars, and boiler plates from the rolling mills. Pittsburgh was on the threshold of its Iron and Steel Age, and was already alive with Irish and Italian immigrants working the mills, and with the riots and strikes of the town's industrial growing pains.

Jamming the river banks were rafts piled high with timber for the shipyards, drab barges loaded with coal and granite-ware, puffing stern-wheeler tugboats filled with iron and glass products, and glittering side-wheel packets complete with red-carpeted staterooms, central salon, and gold scroll saw ornament. And not far back from the noisy, bustling rivers, along the streets of the lower Triangle and of Old Allegheny, were rising great hodgepodge mansions, symbols of vast coal and iron and glass fortunes. Typical, was the imposing pile of stone built by John H. Schoenberger at 425 Penn Avenue, which housed Pittsburgh's earliest private art collection, and may have been of interest to Blythe.

The new Monongahela House rose out of the ashes of the Great Fire of 1845 to match pace with the growth and prosperity of the town. Heavily carved walnut furniture was in the bedrooms, velvet draped the high, narrow windows, and it had china washbasins. It quite displaced the exclusive Exchange Hotel as Pittsburgh's most fashionable hostelry.

From Market Street, once the hub of the town, business was spreading out in all directions. Hogg's Pond had been filled with dirt in leveling Grant's Hill and no longer hindered the city's growth to the west. A new Federal Courthouse was begun in 1853 on the site of the present Park Building. L-shaped Lafayette Hall, where the Republicans were to hold, shortly, their first national convention, went up on the corner of Wood and Fourth.

Even in 1850 Pittsburgh was a city of bridges. A fine new one, outshining the others, spanned the Allegheny at Hand Street, now Ninth Street. It was a cause of great pride and the scene of much gaiety, for the roof carried a promenade, where the élite of society—and Blythe—delighted to stroll. To add to the wonders of such progress, the streets, hotels, and stores "blazed" with gas illumination. The night watch, revived in 1836, was still active when Blythe came back to Pittsburgh, and the watchman stopped below the gas lamps to call the hours. As a matter of fact, Blythe painted one picture called *The Town Crier*.

Not only had the city expanded in size, thrusting outward in all directions with new buildings and bridges, and pushing skyward its smokestacks, water towers, and coal tipples, but it had grown in population—from about 20,000 in 1840 to nearly 50,000 by 1860—and it had changed racially. Hundreds of Irish and South Europeans came after 1851. Beggars were frequent on the streets; in fact, there was a "beggars' court" on Enoch Street, complete with monkeys and organ-grinders. Little ragamuffins roamed the dark, cluttered alleys, out for mischief; and older hoodlums roved the narrow, muddy streets in gangs. One may find their faces peering from many Blythe pictures. And at this time lower Wylie Avenue already had

WHOA EMMA!
(Mrs. James D. Hailman, Pittsburgh, Pa.)

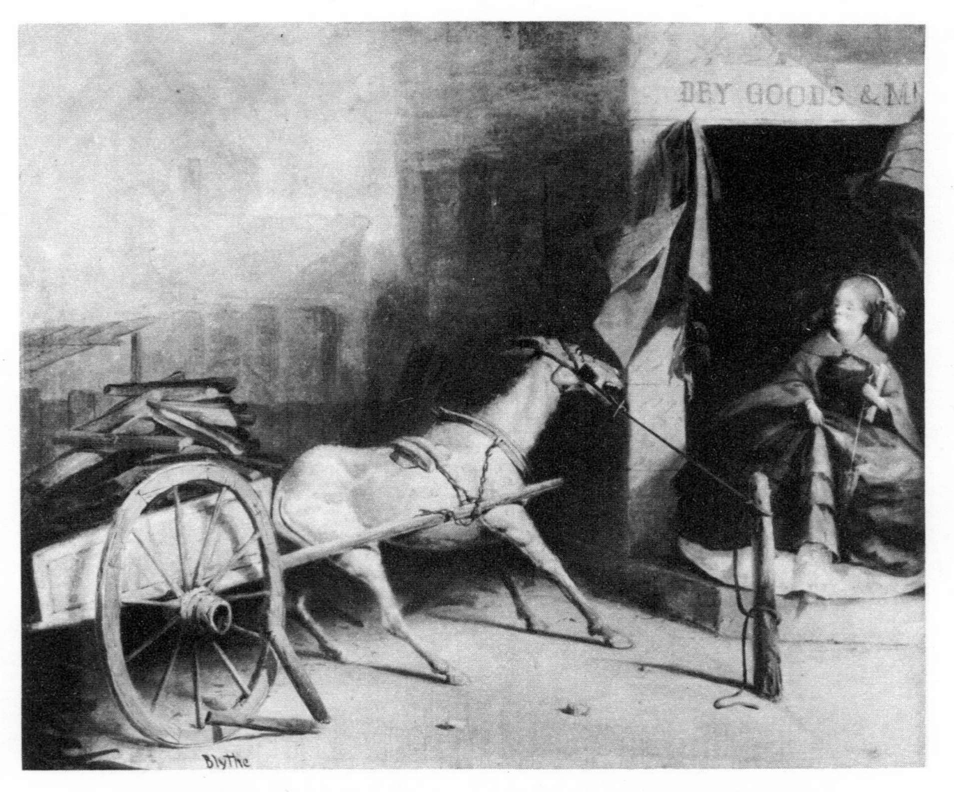

DRY GOODS AND NOTIONS (Duquesne Club, Pittsburgh, Pa.)

so many negroes it was called "Hayti." The rough hillsides of the town made excellent hideouts for fugitive slaves, and Pittsburgh's reputation as an important underground station was established. Blythe had a chance to see the negro of that day. He pictured him in several paintings.

Besides its military and political figures, Pittsburgh had a number of other interesting personalities. In the 1850's and 1860's, Henry Ward Beecher occasionally stormed into town with his oratorical explosions. Young Andrew Carnegie and his associates were expanding their enterprises and rapidly rising to power in the coal and iron industries. Stephen Foster, who now and then joined his friends at Gillespie's, was writing songs and his townsmen were singing them.

At Gillespie's, too, Blythe renewed his friendship with old acquaintances and found, as well, a new group of young artists gathering there. Albert L. Dalbey and J. Warren Fisk were beginning to show great promise as young portrait painters. George Hetzel, fresh from Dusseldorf, was sketching landscapes in company with Alfred Wall. Blythe's old friend, James Reid Lambdin, whom he had known in his apprentice days, now had become one of Pittsburgh's most prominent painters and was hurrying in and out of town on important portrait commissions. Jaspar Lawman had graduated from the rank of scenery painter at Old Drury and was soon to leave for Paris for study under Couture. Russell Smith and W. C. Wall were busy, painting scenes along Pittsburgh's rivers. Young Emil Foerster, who ultimately painted more than 600 portraits of his townsmen after training at Dusseldorf and Frankfurt, John Donaghy, and Otto Krebs were also among the artists who met daily at Gillespie's. It was a lively, versatile group, and Blythe probably learned much from them and entered wholeheartedly into their discussions. We know that Blythe was a regular visitor to Gillespie's after his return to Pittsburgh and that Gillespie often exhibited his paintings in the store windows.

This brief glance into the past has been given to suggest the industrial, cultural, and social life that highlighted mid-nineteenth century Pittsburgh. This life is the backdrop against which Blythe, for a decade, played an eccentric and unique role. That that role was eccentric and unique is known only through his paintings and through tales that have been handed down from generation to generation. To reconstruct Blythe's life during this period, we have little to go on except these and circumstantial evidence from the background in which he lived and worked. Even the little rooms where he lodged and painted long ago were destroyed in the building of skyscrapers. During the years 1856-1857 Blythe lived at Bernard House, a small unpretentious hotel. The next year he moved to the Ashland Hotel, at 97 Fourth Avenue. He must have spent some part of the next three years in East Liverpool, for that address appeared in the index of the Pittsburgh Art Association Catalogue of 1859. From 1861 until his death in 1865, he lived and painted at 66 Third Avenue. In the interim he maintained a studio or residence—probably it was both—in the Denny Building on Fourth Avenue. This was the setting for Blythe's self-portrait, *Art Versus Law,* which came out of his eviction for nonpayment of rent. The painting brought Blythe thirty-five dollars, which probably paid the rent for a few weeks. C. H. Wolff, who then had one of the best art collections in Pittsburgh and who bought the painting from Blythe, has jotted in his ledger: "This work portrays a true incident in the life of the artist when occupying a studio in the Denny Building, corner of Market and Fourth, Pittsburgh. His own form and suggestive features are admirably given. Poor Blythe; all knew his faults—few his virtues."

Chapter Four

COURTROOM SCENES – INTERIORS LANDSCAPES – URCHINS

IN DESCRIBING and analyzing Blythe's Pittsburgh paintings, it seems best to group them according to theme rather than chronology or style. In the first place, it is very difficult to date many of Blythe's paintings; except for the Civil War pictures and one or two others, it is almost impossible to place a painting at the beginning or the end of the short nine-year period that he spent in Pittsburgh. Second, after 1855 Blythe's style is especially uneven and undergoes little marked change or development; Blythe's style alters with his moods rather than the years, and his quality of painting with his subjects rather than with growing skill.

Among the most powerful of Blythe's Pittsburgh paintings is a unique trilogy which has for its theme *law* and *justice.* In one, it is the corruption of lawyers; in the second, the stupidity and indifference of judges and juries; in the third, the seizure of the law by mob violence and rule. These paintings represent Blythe's closest approach to Daumier's satire on the courts; they are his strongest criticism of society; they are his frankest advocacy of reform. And as such, they have kinship in style and theme with Daumier and Hogarth.

In 1856 Blythe wrote a poem-letter to his old Uniontown friend, Hugh A. Gorley, then in Vermont. The letter is concerned with political issues, and is unusually bitter, its substance wholly unseasoned by the humor generally found in Blythe's writings. The last three verses show the extent of Blythe's resentment against corruption and injustice. At first he lashes out at the Press and the Church:

> The press, that mighty monster lever,
> Which shakes things like a western fever,
> Of which truth and truth alone
> Should be the fulcrum, scarcely one,
> except, perhaps, your own, but's gone
>   Astray from it.
> And yet the world looks on and cries
>   "What's the odds?"
> An editor has as good a right as any-
> Body else to make an honest penny.

[Is this a reference to his experience in Indiana?]

> One-half our pulpits are too chuck
> Full of vain, empty-headed truck
> Ambitious only to have a stuck-
> Up congregation to preach to, and
> Ten thousand or so at their command.

[Then he turns his attack on the courts.]

> Our courts with few exceptions
> Are fit subjects for like objections.
> Public opinion first, Blackstone second,
> Now-a-days. And then our juries,
> Oh, if there's such a thing as "furies"
> Why don't they pitch in? Curious,

Just imagine twelve ignoramuses
With flat heads and red "wammuses"
Sitting in judgement on an intricate
Case of law. Beautiful, isn't it?
Boots.—

His three paintings seem to be the pictorial dramatization of his verse. In them Justice, herself, is on trial; Blythe is the prosecuting attorney. The evils he saw—the corruption and weakness of the courts and the miscarriages of justice—he highlights and holds up for all to see.

In the *Lawyer's Dream* Blythe has painted a dozing lawyer slumped in his chair, his long legs crossed on the table before him. Floor and table are littered with law documents and law-books. *The Daily* and the *Iron City* are scattered over the table; on the floor a volume of *Blackstone*—Blythe's symbol of law and justice—is shackled with chain and lock, and other volumes—*Modern Justice* is one—have been flung contemptuously aside. Behind the sleeping figure capers a little black devil with orange eyes, delighting in his master's—or perhaps his slave's—disregard for law and justice and truth. In the background, a wine-colored curtain drawn aside reveals the lawyer's dream sketched in faint outlines. Beyond an American flag, a statesman, over whom hovers an angel bearing a crown, is addressing a legislature. This, evidently, is the aspiration of the fraudulent jurist—a legislative post to crown his career of bribery and dishonesty. It is not clear whether Blythe had a particular member of the bar in mind or is lashing out at what he thought general corruption. The painting is unusual because of its abundance of color—the rich red of the curtain, the vividness of the flag, the golden haze shrouding the dream. In other ways it is typical of Blythe. The fondness for leading the observer to hunt among the deep shadows for partly hidden objects and to explore dark nooks for the artist's symbolisms appears frequently in later paintings.

Courtroom Scene—a second law picture—is a superb example of Blythe's work. In it he shows the inefficiency and incompetence of a jury. The members of the jury have faces of scoundrels and idiots, scallywags and ignoramuses. Some gawk at the ranting prosecutor with blank faces and bulging eyes. Some scowl with distorted grimaces of contemptuous indifference. Some doze, unaware of their responsibilities. Of the same breed is the constable, a bored, hardened old character, who stands by the judge's bench. The judge himself seems to be drifting off into a nap. The accused, entrusted to the wisdom and intelligence of this court, is on the witness stand, a small, wretched, meek figure, who stares at the jury, hopeless. The prosecutor is pointing one bony finger vindictively at the accused and rapping another bejeweled finger at a page of a lawbook on the table. The room is shoddy and dismal, the right setting for the theme of the painting; the plaster is cracked and the brick of the wall shows through in jagged patches. What Blythe says is unmistakable. And there is a forthrightness and strength in its technical treatment, a simplicity, a careful elimination of details, a freedom of brushwork which suit the boldness of the theme.

The third of these paintings is another "trial" or "court" scene, but in this, the jury is self-appointed, justice is administered by a mob. The painting deals with one of the Molly Maguire trials. The "Mollies" were a secret organization of miners who fought in devious and often violent ways against what they thought unfair practices by the mine operators of the Philadelphia and Reading Railroad mining subsidiary. Though recent research by the University of Pennsylvania into four hundred documents in the P&R file dealing with the "Mollies" has led to some doubt that such societies existed in the middle 1800's, Molly Maguire became a synonym for violence, murder, and labor strife. The "Mollies" were undoubtedly a bitter and controversial subject discussed on water front and in factory and tavern across the state; and in the painting Blythe entered vigorously into the discussions. Such a subject gave his caricaturing brush full sway. He paints the Molly Maguires as hoodlums of all types and degrees. In a shack they cluster, hard-faced and grim, with rifles, pistols, and cutlasses at hand. The prisoner sits whittling, held fast by a chain about his ankles. Around him a mob is engaged in playing cards and lounging about while they listen to the harangue of a spokesman, who pounds a table and waves his fist in the air. From a technical standpoint, the composition hangs together well because of the interplay of light and shadows and because of the arrangement of the many figures. Color is keyed low to a mood, grim and somewhat sinister.

Like the Dutch and Flemish painters, Blythe liked to paint interiors. One of these is the interior of Bobbie Burn's cottage. From his Scottish father Blythe may have learned as a boy to read Burn's poetry, and to know that he liked poetry, although what he wrote himself was chiefly doggerel. It is not surprising that quite sympathetically he paints Burns in his "auld clay biggen," a melancholy man, seated, chin in hand, in the center of the room. He is alone except for a tiny mouse crouching behind his chair. The plank floor, wooden beams, and wall paneling gave Blythe a chance to use his favorite browns, and the open fireplace let him paint the golden glow that is so often in his pictures. On the wall hang the poet's plaid tam and cape, and scrawled on the door is "Ellisland, June 1788." Books, a desk, a jug, barrels, a stool, a keg, and farm implements are about the room. Possibly the moodiness and loneliness of Blythe, himself, is reflected in the painting; Blythe and Burns had qualities in common. But the painting is too posed, too lacking in life, to be among Blythe's best; Blythe is at his best when he paints activity and groups of people and moments of robust humor.

The Fireside in the Duquesne Club collection radiates more warmth than the Burns. Many objects—baskets, cups, saws, horseshoes, utensils, tools—hang on the wall and litter the floor. A deep red cape hangs from a hook. A man, two women, and a little boy are seated before a glowing fire and an open door shows a young man and a girl sitting close together in a large chair. In the picture is cheerful family life, much, perhaps, as Blythe had known it in his boyhood. The obvious tinge of nostalgia does not degenerate into sentimentality.

Family life less harmonious is shown by Blythe in another interior. With something of the color and vigor of the elder Brueghel, Blythe has painted, very dramatically, the *Return of the Prodigal.* He has taken liberties with the Biblical version. Instead of the fatted calf, the father seems to be greeting his son with curses. The father is dressed in a bright blue coat, a red hat, and baggy brown knickers. He scowls and waves a club over the prodigal's head. The elder brother has joined him; he brandishes a stool. The figures are grouped in a balanced composition; the prodigal has the central position, with his back to the observer; the father, held back by a daughter, tries to lunge at the boy from the left; the brother, held back by the mother, swings at the boy from the right. Because there are unusually bright dashes of color, and the painting is unsigned, some art critics doubt that Blythe painted the picture. The mother wears a red jacket, the sister a red skirt, the prodigal blue trousers and a green jacket. A splash of blood spurts from a gash on the side of his head. The brilliance of the coloring is accentuated by the deep brown shadows of the room, pierced only by a daub of pale sky through the open doorway.

People interested Blythe far more than fields and valleys, even though he had spent his boyhood on a farm in the pleasant, fertile slopes of Ohio. He did not paint many landscapes, yet one of these, the *General Doubleday Crossing the Potomac,* painted during the Civil War, is considered by many to be his best painting. Much less important are two small companion pictures—perhaps of the Blythe farm, painted during a visit home sometime in the 1850's. They hang in the home of his nephew, Heber H. Blythe, in East Liverpool. One of them, the *Man Eating in Field,* shows a farmer lying under a haystack. Beside him are a big basket, a tin cup, some cutlery. The fields fade away in a sombre yellow haze of wheat. Gray sky threatens a coming storm; the Blythe browns are everywhere. In the *Harvesting,* a man and a woman stand in the foreground. The man, wiping his forehead, holds a scythe; the girl wears a red dress and carries a large basket on her arm. Far off, two men are raking. The fields, dotted with haystacks, slope away toward the big barn and house. The sky is a cloudy, pearl-gray, and the whole scene—fields, trees, buildings, figures—is bathed in shadowy green and brown tones. Neither of the two paintings is distinguished in color, drawing, or composition. They are done adequately, are mildly interesting, but they never approach the *General Doubleday.*

A third minor landscape, attributed to Blythe, and originally owned by Blythe's friend and fellow artist John Donaghy of Pittsburgh, has aroused interest because of speculation as to what scene it shows. It may be the old Wilkin's homestead in Pittsburgh, although the suggestion has been made that it is a view on the Blythe farm near East Liverpool. A brown shack stands overlooking a stream. Gray-green hills, with a few trees on them, slope up past a stone wall to a large house at the top of the hill—a grayish, red-roofed house of considerable size. The sky is a troubled mixture of grays which evaporate into a golden haze. The brush strokes are broad and free, the details lost in vagueness; the coloring is soft and cool. Its atmospheric quality gives the landscape merit beyond the other two.

The *General Doubleday* is not only one of Blythe's best paintings, but is close to the best American landscapes. It was painted in the summer of 1863, soon after news reached Pittsburgh of Doubleday's having crossed a shallow turn in the Potomac, June 8, 1863, on his march towards Gettysburg. During Blythe's camp-follower days with the Thirteenth Pennsylvania Regiment early in the War, those same troops had crossed the Potomac four times within a few weeks. Naturally, the memory of Patterson and Doubleday's men winding over the green hills of Maryland stayed in Blythe's mind. In the *General Doubleday* there is the stream of men winding down the valley to the river and curving up over the cool, hazed slopes that fade into the mistiness of the distant foothills. Blythe is more than illustrator or cartoonist here; he is a master painter in the best landscape tradition—sensitive to effects of light and air, to balance and relation of parts, to color and the vibration of action. But besides its great charm and loveliness, the painting is important because it illustrates Blythe's amazing versatility—he was wood carver, portraitist, panoramist, genre painter—and increases the mystery of how a self-taught artist could, at times, paint brilliantly.

Blythe's landscapes are uneven in quality, but the urchin theme which he painted so often shows an even wider range. These paintings are of so many types and many levels of quality and interest. There are those of ugly, ragged toughies and blank-faced morons, some rather dull and lifeless, others like *Newsboys* and *Sleigh Ride* rather lively and interesting.

Then there are the schoolboys, usually single figures, rather animated, well drawn, highly finished, and admirable in modelling and flesh tones. To be sure, none has the sentimentality of J. G. Brown's sweet-faced cherubs, but they are never among Blythe's best work. Why Blythe was so interested in these subjects is not clear. It is true the theme was popular among illustrators of Blythe's time; George H. Coneghy's pictures in periodicals are typical. These illustrations may have led Blythe to try his hand at the same sort of thing. Being Blythe, he put on canvas the youngsters he saw haggling over pennies and puffing cigars under the gas lamps of Cherry Alley, and the boys he remembered about the country schools when he had gone back to East Liverpool.

Among the more mediocre of these urchin paintings is one called *Spilt Milk*, or, sometimes, *The Idiot.* A very blank-faced boy is sitting on the floor. He has tipped a bowl in one hand and splatters his face with milk from it by holding a spoon above his head.

Yet the same Blythe who wasted his talents on a painting like *Spilt Milk* could paint the *Newsboys,* which, though far from his best work, is well drawn and interesting in composition. In it, two hard-faced young toughies, one ragged and puffing a cigar, haggle over their earnings. That they are newsboys is suggested—Blythe is apt to be over-obvious—by the *Journal* and *Daily Dispatch* beside them on a newsstand. Each boy grips some coins in his dirty hand.

In the *Firecracker,* owned by the Duquesne Club, a round-faced lad is trying to light a large cigar with a firecracker. A hat is cocked on his head, and under his arm are books and a slate scribbled with this interesting combination: "Blythe," "Boots," "H. Clay," and "1856," the 1856 probably dating the painting. Blythe seldom gives a date; generally one must guess it from theme or style.

What may have been intended as a companion painting to the *Firecracker* is the *Street Urchin,* recently bought by the Butler Art Institute. A little boy is kneeling to light a firecracker with a cigar. At least eight companions look on; the exact number is difficult to count—eight heads are clear, but there are also hands and arms that may belong to unseen boys on the outer edges of the group. They are all huddled on the curb beneath a lamppost. In the lower right-hand corner is the suggestion of a barrel. Edges of kegs and barrels are common in Blythe's paintings. One wonders if he intends them for local color or merely for filling up the corners of the paintings.

Besides the *Firecracker,* the Duquesne Club owns the *Urchin.* He is a snub-nosed, curly-headed, ragged boy, who nibbles on a straw and kneels beside a wicker basket. The drawing is like the *Firecracker* boy, and in it, too, the color is scaled down to the typical grays and browns. Very like the *Urchin* is *Corn Fed,* in the same collection. The youngster is chewing on an ear of corn. His straw hat and nondescript suit are sketched casually in grays and browns.

More illustrative in treatment, and of greater interest, are two paintings undoubtedly painted during one of Blythe's visits to East Liverpool. Both are owned by Mr. H. N. Harker of East Liverpool. Probably the scenes are East Liverpool scenes. The first is the *Sleigh Ride.* This title is misleading; *Sled Ride* would be more exact, for in the painting a sled with five screaming, clutching boys aboard whizzes down a winding hill, racing past houses on the right, a watering trough and two boys on the left. Other sleds come racing down the hill, and two boys are sprawled grotesquely on the track by their capsized sled. Except for the dash of a red scarf, the scene is a cold gray and white. It exudes a kind of haziness and bleakness that is numbing. One almost expects to see his own frosted breath; the spirit of the action is vividly given.

The Truant Boy, also in the Harker Collection, shows in profile a schoolmaster seated at a tall, wooden desk. The mother of the truant, wrapped in a shawl, sits with her back to the observer, seemingly in an attitude of angry shame. The truant stands on one foot, tracing marks with a finger on the wooden bench. In his attitude is some defiance, though he does not look at his mother or the schoolmaster. For background, a draped window frames the schoolmaster's desk, and dimly the school children are suggested. The composition is good, the colors warm with the usual deep browns and occasional tones of olive green and deep red, and the attitude and the expression of all three figures are skillfully shown.

There are two paintings of little schoolboys which are more maturely painted than any of the other urchin paintings. One is called *Mischief Maker.* The boy sits on a bench before his desk whittling the edge of it with a penknife, the spelling book in his other hand ignored. Propped in front of him are his slate with a few scribbled figures on it, and a closed book. The rough planks of desk and bench are carved with initials. In *On the Sly* the same type of round-faced youngster sits before his desk. He has raised a *United States Spelling Book* to the side of his face to hide his munching of a piece of raisin bread. One elbow rests on a paper-backed book. On the desk are an inkwell, his lunch basket, and his hat. For color and style, *Boy Eating Watermelon,* should be grouped with the two schoolboy figures. A little boy in a straw hat sits, a watermelon on his lap. His right hand holds a large slice he bites into; his left holds a knife. About him are scattered rinds and seeds. In all three paintings the flesh color is remarkably clear and the features well modelled, the figures drawn with a feeling for anatomy yet not burdened with over-detail. They have something of the maturity and polish of Blythe's best portraits.

Youth and the Sugar Bowl and its companion piece—the companion piece is lost—apparently try to preach a sermon. Agnes Way's *Scrapbook,* a very valuable collection of art clippings taken from Pittsburgh newspapers of the late 1800's, seldom notes dates or exact sources, but one clipping in it gives details of these paintings:

Two paintings by Blythe are attracting much attention. They are the property of Judge Acheson, and are among the very best efforts of the queer old fellow [Blythe], whose oddities are remembered by middle-aged Pittsburghers. One painting shows an innocent-faced, curly headed child in the act of pilfering sugar from a bowl that stands on the table. The companion work reveals the blear-eyed countenance of a hardened old reprobate peering from the square formed by the bars of a jail door. The two extremes are here most strikingly shown. The first theft, and result. A life of dishonesty stretches between the two scenes, and the hardened features of the man find a resemblance in those of the child.

The painting of the child eventually became the property of the Spang family of Pittsburgh, and then was given to Mr. John A. Harper, a prominent banker and a friend of Blythe's. It is now owned by his daughters, Mrs. H. A. Byram and Mrs. Franklin C. Irish. The picture is a large one—22″ × 26″—and an interesting one. The flesh tones, the texture of the gray-tan ragged clothes, and the battered yellow straw hat the child wears, the modelling of the glass bowl of sugar, and the suggestion of a knife, plate, cup and saucer on the table against a sombre background are done in the manner of the Flemish and Dutch—warm, mellow, and pleasing. Perhaps *Old Man Peering from Jail* will eventually turn up to complete the story and add to the interest of the first painting.

All these paintings of children show a variety of techniques and an amazing difference of quality. They range from the dull, mediocre urchin pictures to the better drawn and more interesting compositions developed in the sledding and schoolmaster ones and the even better watermelon boy and the two schoolboys. The explanation of their differences is not difficult to find; Blythe's paintings vary because of his temperament—his restlessness, his indifference to money and praise, and his occasional outbursts of enthusiasm and energy.

Chapter Five

TAVERNS—TRAMPS—STREET SCENES
THE POST OFFICE—THE HORSEMARKET
THE FIRST PRESBYTERIAN CHURCH
SHOPS AND OFFICES

FORMAL PORTRAITS probably bored Blythe. What he really liked was to make "unofficial" and unsolicited portraits of the men who hobnobbed with him in bars and on street corners. One, *Good Times,* is of an old toper swigging from his bottle, a portly old gentleman in olive green, wearing a little black beret-like cap, and seated in a red chair. The jug, too, is greenish. A companion piece is *Hard Times;* the bailiff, pompous, stern, with stick in hand, leads a ragged, unhappy-looking tramp towards a jail. A third of this type is *The Fiddler.* The fiddler faces us, his audience. He wears a green tunic and a flat-brimmed greenish hat. With downcast eyes he plays his fiddle. His face is made almost grotesque by his very large nose. In all three of these there are no background details; Blythe has set the drab and pathetic figures against deep sombre tones of gray and brown.

In *The Drinker* a man leans on a great keg, drinking from a glass. He is a typical Blythe character, hard-faced and sour,

PITTSBURGH HORSEMARKET (Mrs. R. Lucien Patton, Ligonier, Pa.)

POST OFFICE
(Carnegie Institute, Pittsburgh, Pa.)

and is painted in the broad sweeping brush strokes of Hals or Manet. The color of the drink is red, suggesting wine rather than beer, yet a stein is on a round keg. A possible companion piece to this scene is *The Temperance Pledge,* in which a sad-eyed man, his face highlighted by red and orange tones, stares down at a piece of paper in his hand on which are the words "Temperance Pledge." The neck of a green bottle shows in the lower left corner of the painting. The shirt of the man, whose head and shoulders only are seen, is orange-brown, the scarf blue. Pittsburgh was feeling, in Blythe's time, the impact of the "Washingtonians," the "Marthas," "The Sons of Temperance," and other crusading groups. Thousands vowed to reform after hearing the orations of William Lloyd Garrison, Wendell Phillips, and others who preached the evils of strong drink from the platform of Temperance Hall on the corner of Smithfield and Diamond. Blythe makes, in this picture, his comment on the crusades.

The Historical Society of Western Pennsylvania owns a Blythe given it by Mrs. Frank C. Osburn. This may be the lost *Conviviality* lent by Peter Brady to the Pittsburgh Library Exhibit of 1879. Two men sit at a table crowded with glasses and jugs, smoking their pipes. A third man—toothless, grinning, old—hunches over a keg, filling his pipe. The deep brown shadows yield just the outlines of other jugs on a shelf and a picture on a wall. The sombre greens, grays, and browns of the recesses of the room contrast with the dull reds and green-blues of the men's clothes. There can be little doubt the painting was copied from *Interior of a Public House* by David Teniers, the Younger, now in the Cleveland Museum but was not in this country at the time Blythe painted his picture. Blythe's varies from Teniers' only in size, color, and a few minor details. Why he digresses from his usual originality is not clear—perhaps to see if he could match Teniers, perhaps merely for fun or for some special purpose not clear to us today. It does prove that Blythe saw prints of European painters and was influenced by them. A small painting of a tavern scene, recently discovered in the McGirr Collection, probably done by Blythe and bought from him at the time four others in the collection were bought, adds more proof. The subject and composition were obviously suggested by paintings of Teniers or Ostade. Prints of paintings like Teniers' *Boors Carousing* (Wallace Collection), *Players at Backgammon* (National Gallery, London), *Two Peasants Playing Cards* (Liechtensteingalerie, Vienna), or *Boors Smoking and Drinking* (Freiherrn Heyl Zu Herrnsheim Collection, Worms) may have suggested the theme and the arrangement and drawing of some figures and objects.

Blythe treats drinking with no attempt at moralizing and with tolerant amusement at its pleasures. It is interesting that in his verse Blythe attacks drunkenness with great venom. In the second stanza of a poem called *A Pen Sketch of a Drunkard* Blythe writes:

> Out from the cold, blank emptiness
> Of a drunkard's home, slowly and hushed as
> A gnome shade vomited from the green pestilent
> Stomach of a sepulchre, comes forth a thing
> The suppliant tongue of charity might
> Hesitate to call a man.

And in the final stanza Blythe gives us this description:

> His eyes like angry, ill-closed, half-healed
> Wounds physicianless, and cheek like blood-dipt
> Violets mirrored 'gainst the broad blue sky . . .
> He wakes; and like the raven in the pallid
> Bust of Pallas, falls the light in yellow
> Flakes upon his livid cheek, simmering
> On his parched, disfigured face,
> Made such by his own debauchery.

In the *Drunkard's Doom* Blythe traces his downfall " . . . step by step, and drink by drink, Until he sees his body sink into its loathsome tomb." He ends the poem dramatically:

> The rest's soon told—crime's putrid wave
> Soon sweeps him from the earth,
> His wife's in heaven, his boy's a slave,
> Himself in a forgotten grave,
> His soul in Hell.

One wonders which—painting or verse—expressed Blythe's true feeling. Or is each true at a different time?

Blythe shows great delight in painting grimaces. Many times he paints large, round, misshapen heads and faces with beady eyes, bulbous noses, twisted mouths, and ugly scowls. In this he is much like Goya and Ostade and Brouwer. There is no uglier grimace, though, than that which distorts the face of the man in *Man Putting on Boots.* So deep are the browns and the shadows that the man's face is partially obscured; but there is no mistaking his rage as he struggles to get his boots on. He seems cursing the boots, their maker, and the steer that produced the leather.

Of Blythe's character sketches none is better than *The Shoremen.* It has skillful drawing and color, emphasis by form and mass, casual and free brushwork, and keen characterization. The figures strongly suggest Forain. The background is the high brick wall and board fence of a warehouse on the river's edge. Two tramps are slouched in earnest, secretive conversation. The younger is painted in varying tones of brown; the old-timer in grays and black. The wall and fence are drab tan, but the sky is a flash of pale blue. An interesting touch is the crudely scrawled human figure on the wall, rather like the figures scratched on the slates of Blythe's schoolboys. The painting is an example of Blythe's matured skill and insight.

A very amusing and excellent painting is *Whoa Emma.* Emma, a sleepy-eyed old nag is plodding across a narrow, plank bridge, not at all aware that she is about to step into an opening in the planks and fall into the stream. And unaware, too, are her riders, a skinny old negro in a large straw hat, and his fat wife perched up behind him, a pipe between her teeth and an umbrella over her head. Emma suggests Don Quixote's Rocinante as pictured by Daumier. This is Blythe at his best, full of humor, skillful in drawing, casual and free in brush strokes, and catching the essence of the situation with few details.

This delightful painting of the ways of the negro raises the speculation why Blythe never illustrated a Foster song or painted a Foster character. *Camp Town Races* or *O Susanna* fit well into the rollicking, lighthearted spirit that so often possessed Blythe. There is no evidence that Blythe and Foster knew each other. Foster was eleven years younger, only a boy of seven or eight when Blythe was in Pittsburgh serving his apprenticeship to Joseph Woodwell. In the fifties, during Blythe's second stay in Pittsburgh, Foster was in Cincinnati for a time; and he went to New York in 1860, where he lived until his death in 1864, one year before Blythe's. It is, therefore, not likely that their association was close even if they did meet at Gillespie's. Perhaps Blythe's independent nature kept him aloof, even from Foster with whom he could have had much in common. Blythe went his own way, painting only his own feelings and observations.

A mule dominates another of Blythe's most delightful paintings. In *Dry Goods and Notions,* a mule rears back against his cart, upsetting the cordwood piled on it. The cause of his agitation is a pompous and dignified woman in crinoline and mantle coming from a dry goods store on Market Street. Her dress is a deep gray satin; her gloves are green. Offended,

THE HIDEOUT (William H. Vodrey, East Liverpool, O.)

STAGE COACH
(Duquesne Club, Pittsburgh, Pa.)

she stares haughtily at the snickering mule. A dash of red, yellow, and green is in the cloth that waves by the doorway, and on the lintel is lettered "Dry Goods and Mil . . ." Paintings of this type suggest that Blythe might have been very successful as a cartoonist. He caught truth through exaggeration; he looked at the world as Cruikshank and Johnston did.

In *The Runaway* Blythe painted the antics of a horse. The horse has reared on his hindlegs, upsetting the carriage and dumping on the ground the driver, who sprawls face downward, one boot shooting off into space, and the woman, who is all but lost in a cloud of dust; only one of her legs is clear, immodestly exposed to the knee! Her parasol, gloves, and bonnet are flying through the air. The horse has lost a shoe, but he rolls his eyes in devilish glee. The coloring is reduced to browns against a glowing orange background. The explosive motion of it all—the clouds of dust, the broken wheels, the flying objects—is masterfully suggested.

Generally, Blythe was not particularly gallant towards women. He usually catches a situation in which they appear ridiculous. *The Washerwoman* is an exception. She bends over a brown tub set on a heavy stool, a sturdy, self-reliant person. She wears a gray hat, a gray waist, a brown skirt. It is an uncluttered composition in sombre brown and gray that suit the placid, homely subject.

Little known are two small paintings, companion pieces. The first shows a man and wife kneeling in prayer beside a table. Behind them, a little boy waves his hat at a goat which is poking its head in at the doorway. The second shows the couple now sprawled on the floor, the table cover dangling from the edge of the table, a pie scattered on the floor, and the goat scurrying out the door. Unfortunately, age has so darkened the sombre tones that the original full-bodied humor of the situation is blurred.

The Hunter and *The Town Crier* each shows a single figure. In the first, the hunter, his gun under his arm, stops at a crossroads to study a sign which reads "East Liverpool." The painting, the colors of which are a limited range of greens and browns, is undistinguished except for its unusually fluent and broad brush strokes. *The Town Crier* shows a large, muscular man with a red scarf knotted about his neck, backed against a dusky building on which is a sign "Lager and Pretzels" and "Varieties." The night watch had been revived in Pittsburgh in 1836. The members of the force were armed with clubs, not only to enforce order, but to signal to each other by beating the clubs upon the pavement. In the painting, the figure is the personification of majestic dignity. Perhaps he once guided Blythe homeward in the small hours of the morning, and so is painted as a gentleman of real distinction!

Painted in much the same style is *Ole Cezer,* recently discovered at the home of Mrs. William Reed Thompson of Pittsburgh. In rich browns and oranges Blythe paints Cezer, a decrepit negro, coming up out of a cellarway carrying a tub of whitewash. Irregularly scrawled on the wall: "Whitewash don heir" and "Ole cloves Bot and Sold."

The Gouty Fisherman is a typically Blythe-distorted figure, posed in a dark, cluttered interior. The fisherman in a lounging robe sits in a large chair with his back to the fireplace, a rather elaborate one with fire screen, bellows, carved mantelpiece. Before him is an enormous tub brimming with water out of which tiny fishtails dart. He is leaning forward, solemnly intent on hooking one of the fish with the line dangling from his long pole. About him are a creel, fish rods, many kinds of flies, a mounted fish, a net. His foot propped on a gout kettle and the table crowded with medicine at his elbow help explain the title. Just which gouty Pittsburgher this is, who substitutes a tub filled with minnows for the water of the

Ohio below the Point, which teems with catfish and carp, cannot be determined.

There are two paintings probably painted during Blythe's Pittsburgh period which do not use Pittsburgh persons or settings. They are like his other Pittsburgh paintings in color and brushwork, if not in theme. One is of Don Quixote, a subject unique for Blythe. Don Quixote wears green knickers and red hose and reclines easily in a chair, illustrating with sweeping gestures what he is saying to Sancho. Sancho, a squat little fellow, stands solidly before his master, hat in hand. His vest is fawn colored with dark sleeves, his knickers black, his leggings fawn. The coloring is characteristic of Blythe, especially in the generous sprinkling of dark reds and greens in drapery and rug as well as in figures and in the dark brown shadowy background. On the wall are shield and sword, and on the floor beside Don Quixote's chair are pieces of armour and two heavy, studded volumes, all well modelled. The figure of the knight, himself, is slim and graceful, suggesting that possibly Blythe is following Doré. The Doré illustrations were widely known; the circumstantial evidence is strong that Blythe borrowed his idea. This is the only painting in which Blythe has drawn his subject from literature.

The second painting is more difficult to identify or interpret. The principal figure is a tramp, quite possibly an Irish immigrant; for the stick under his arm could be a shillalah, a clay pipe is between his teeth, and he wears a peaked hat. The setting is unquestionably some seaport town, perhaps one Blythe visited in his Navy days. Faintly outlined in the misty background is a masted schooner, but the ensign cannot be identified. Sharing the central position with the tramp is a lifesize cigar store Indian standing at the entrance to a tobacco warehouse. Since cigar store Indians were originally fashioned by New England carvers of ship figureheads and were to be found in every New England town and village—though to be sure they spread rapidly to other parts of the country—a strong case can be made out for the suggestion that the seaport is a New England one, perhaps Boston, for Blythe knew it well and it was a popular landing point for Irish immigrants. The title, *Land of Liberty,* suggests that this may, indeed, show an immigrant being welcomed to America by the First American. Blythe was fond of symbolism; he may well have used the cigar store Indian in this way. If this is the meaning Blythe intended, the immigrant's welcome is not a particularly warm one; the Indian regards him with disdain, although he seems reluctantly to extend to him a long pipe, possibly an indication that since the immigrant is now in America the time has come to smoke the pipe of peace. The painting is an interesting one, more for the questions it raises than for its technique. The figures are typically Blythe—mildly distorted, with tiny feet, clenched fists, rather stiff pose; Blythe often used the combination of fences, warehouse walls, cellar doorways, scattered bricks, and hazy, cloudy sky beyond.

The painting was bought from J. J. Gillespie by C. H. Wolff for the small sum of $35 in the 1860's, and has since passed into other collections.

As time went on, Blythe caught more and more the vivid color and the sharp activity, the flavor and spirit of Pittsburgh; setting and events have more and more the tang of Pittsburgh streets and life. He caught more and more the intensity of mid-nineteenth century America as it went on its highly individual way in a city, partly at least, frontier.

The Pittsburgh Horsemarket makes the old horsemarket come alive again. The bellowings and bickerings and neighings, the smells and actions and colors, the people and animals, all are very real; obviously the man who painted the market had watched it many times. Humor is everywhere—in the indignant glare of the horse who is submitting to a rude inspection of his teeth, in the malicious smirk of another, who in wrath at all mankind, has nipped a boy by the seat of his pantaloons. The scene is Duquesne Way in the neighborhood of Sixth Street, then St. Clair and nicknamed the "battleground" for its noisy activity. The church tower in the background probably is that of Christ Methodist Church, built in 1853 at Penn and Eighth. Or the tower may be that of the Second Presbyterian Church, dedicated in 1858, which stood not far away at Seventh and Penn, and had two towers, one high and Gothic, the other low and much like that in the painting. The drawing deviates slightly from the actual towers, but Blythe occasionally adjusted matters to suit his purpose. The other buildings in the background are too generalized and vaguely outlined to be recognizable. *The Horsemarket* easily is one of Blythe's best. It has all the delightful characteristics of his genre work—humor, vitality, color, flavor, a touch of caricature.

In spite of its lively subject, the colors are scaled down to Blythe's typical tans, heightened by red shirts and splashes of blue. Blythe has deliberately put emphasis on the ridiculous; yet the ridicule is not biting nor does it distort the truth. He watches with amusement; he tells with good humor. One is likely to chuckle and to say: Yes, sir! That's just how it looks!

In 1856 a new Post Office with a great arched doorway stood at the corner of Fifth Avenue and Smithfield Street, where the Park Building is now. Blythe painted its activities with unfailing wit and genial satire in the *Post Office,* now owned by Carnegie Institute. He sees much. Six or seven men and women are jostling one another for a place at the small General Delivery window. Their attitudes are tense and grotesque. A basket has been upset in the crush; a billowy-skirted woman is boring determinedly into the center of the group; a boy, in his efforts to reach the window, has ripped the trousers of the man ahead of him. Five other persons are outside the archway: a ragged, stogie chewer crouching on the steps; a young pickpocket rifling a pocket; two men reading their mail; a third man peering over another's shoulder at a letter.

In the painting Blythe strikes a wider range of color than is usual with him. His typical tans, grays, taupes, fawns, and browns are used, but shades of rose are in the billowing skirt of the woman at the center and deep rose and blue are on her bonnet. Another woman wears a dark green bonnet. Other touches of color are here and there—a red tie, a red jacket, a dark red carpet-bag. White sharpens the newspapers, the letters, the petticoat, and the stocking of the billowy-skirted woman.

Blythe evidently enjoyed the—to him—grotesque, humorous activity under the alcoved arches before the delivery windows, for he painted a second picture, *Gentleman's Delivery Window*. The gentlemen are crowded about, inquiring at the window, peering in their letter boxes, leaning against the wall or the column in the center, absorbed in their reading. The floor is scattered with envelopes. The robust humor, the color, the tang of the other Post Office painting is lacking.

Blythe painted many interiors—churches, taverns, courtrooms, hideouts, cobbler shops, drawing rooms, offices. His tour of the town omitted little; most of the lower Triangle passes in revue.

The stately and fashionable First Presbyterian Church is the setting for a painting newly discovered—*Pittsburgh Piety*. Before a background of pseudo-Gothic arches, the minister, perhaps the Reverend William M. Paxton, from a high, ornate pulpit draped in red and flanked by three-globed lights, stands facing his congregation, probably a distinguished one since the First Church was among the oldest and wealthiest. The restraint, the avoidance of satire or comment, is unusual for Blythe. He has painted the backs of the men and women's heads, instead of caricaturing their faces, as he might be expected to do. The coloring is subdued; it fits the mood. Perhaps Blythe was too good a Scotch Presbyterian to jibe at such a scene; at any rate, he does not caricature.

Blythe painted the hangout of a group of tramps. More than one title has been given this painting, but the usual one is *The Hideout.* Five men are getting ready for the business of the day—panhandling, pickpocketing, and the like. One, in a yellowish suit, sits by the fire eating ham and eggs. Another patches a red cap. A third, in blue, shaves before a propped-up mirror. A fourth, red-shirted, is pouring milk from a jug into a large container, but he has been so disconcerted by the stumbling descent of a fifth man from the loft that he is spilling milk onto the table. As it drips to the floor the cat laps at it. The table is crowded with a basket of food, a fowl, some vegetables, and a string of sausages which dangles over the edge. On the floor near a trunk and barrel lie tossed a pair of down-at-the-heel boots. Ragged clothing hangs over a chair. Stale cigaret butts and scattered playing cards are strewn about. In the obscure shadows done in sombre grays and greens and tans that suggest the dirt and depression of the cluttered room, hangs an end of ham. All this makes a dreary, a rather horrible scene. But Blythe brings the scene alive; and in spite of its jumble of details, the composition hangs together remarkably well because of the distribution of high lights and shadows, masses and forms.

Blythe shows another interior, an office—on January 4, 1859, the wall calendar says—just as a smirking bill collector is handing bills to a gloomy-faced man at his desk. The sheaf of *Posts* on a rack suggest this may be the office of John P. Barr, editor of the *Post.* In another painting, one of his liveliest, *The Democratic Procession,* Blythe showed the editor and the owner peering from a window of the Post Building and cheering as the parade passed. Since *January Bills* is an unhappy occasion, Republican Blythe probably enjoyed picturing Democrat Barr in it.

A shoemaker's shop—it may be that of Blythe's friend, William Blakely, 9 Federal Street—is the interior for *The Cobbler Shop.* A ragged fellow is holding out a boot for repairs. The dim-lit room with the two faces peering out of the darkness, the plank floor, the vague outlines of barrels and tools strongly suggest Dutch genre interiors. Blythe's success with the pathetic figure of the man holding out, hopefully, the worn boot, and the hunched figure of the cobbler, shows why many couple Blythe's name with Ostade and Brouwer.

In a pencil sketch called *William Blakely,* Blythe's cobbler friend stands, a portly gentleman with high hat and cane. Across a corner of the drawing is scrawled "A free-made-man." It is signed "Boots," and has Blythe's initials in script.

Blythe in two pictures shows Pittsburgh citizens how ridiculous they looked climbing onto the crowded stagecoaches that rumbled and bumped over the rutted streets. In *The Stage Coach* a hoop-skirted woman in pink struggles to get inside the coach, though she has caused an exasperated man to spill into the street the vegetables from his large basket. Vague faces show in the shadowy, jammed interior of the coach. Its top is crowded with two little boys, baskets, parcels, and at least three men. Another man is trying to climb on. Still another is handing up a basket to the driver. The colors are confined to the usual grays and tans except for the

PROSPECTING
(Alexander Nimick, Sewickley, Pa.)

RECRUITS WANTED
(Alexander Nimick, Sewickley, Pa.)

pink skirt and red hat of the woman. Again Blythe makes the ludicrous incident alive, not a set tableau or cartoon, and keeps the crowded picture free of cluttering detail.

A Blythe painting lately found by a New York gallery is much like *The Stage Coach* in subject and arrangement, but has more vivid coloring. The lavender of the matron's bustled skirt is almost the color of the skirt of the woman in the *Post Office*.

In *Prospecting*—a small picture—Blythe gives another scene of his times. The painting satirizes the rush from Pittsburgh to Oil City after oil has been discovered and the first well been sunk by Colonel E. L. Drake, on August 27, 1859. An ambitious and optimistic speculator, carrying pack, canteen, and a big bundle marked "green backs," has stopped to study a signpost which advertises for sale lands whose oil will bring millions to the owner. Ankle-deep in mud, he reads the sign. A turtle, a broken barrel of crude oil, the bones of a horse, and the skeleton of a wagon half sunk in a shallow marsh make Blythe's point. The oil lands studded with derricks are the picture's faraway background.

Chapter Six

LINCOLN'S VISIT TO PITTSBURGH IN 1861 OUTBREAK OF THE CIVIL WAR – BLYTHE AND THE PENNSYLVANIA THIRTEENTH WAR PAINTINGS

As Blythe was finishing these paintings, the Civil War was beginning. It widened very suddenly his interests far beyond the Allegheny and Monongahela. Always alive to actions and ideas around him, Blythe for the remaining five years of his life painted war pictures instead of Pittsburgh genre, yet in that time he painted only a dozen or so pictures.

February, 1861, Abraham Lincoln on his way to his inauguration stopped at Pittsburgh. In a downpour, the night of February 14, the President-elect went with great ceremony to the city's best hotel, the Monongahela House. While guns boomed a mighty salute, the Pennsylvania Dragoons, the Jackson Independent Blues, and the Washington Infantry under General J. S. Negley escorted him through the flag-draped streets. That Blythe was one of those who huddled along the store fronts to cheer Lincoln, Blythe's portrait of Lincoln in his *Emancipation Proclamation* and in *The Blair Family* is fair proof.

Within two months of the President's visit, Fort Sumter fell. The President called for volunteers. Pittsburgh was plunged into a fever of mass meetings and recruitings. The district became alive with camps—Camp Wright at Hulton on the Allegheny, Camp Howe in Oakland, and many others —as the young men of Pittsburgh volunteered. The volunteering was so prompt and enthusiastic that twelve days after Fort Sumter the first troops were ready to leave. On April 24 they mustered on the East Common, in Allegheny. Then they plodded in the rain along Western Avenue, Ohio Street, up St. Clair and Fifth Street, to Smithfield, on to Sixth Street, and down to Liberty. In Kier's Warehouse near the station, the troops were feasted and cheered.

Among the troops was the Thirteenth Regiment of Pennsylvania Volunteers, commanded by Colonel T. A. Rowley; and among those who watched was Blythe. The blare and throb of the music, the uniforms, and the emotional farewells seem to have stirred him deeply, for months later he painted *Union Troops Entraining.* He was forty-six years old, too old to enlist but not too old to follow the troops. And follow he did. He went with the Thirteenth to Harrisburg, where the men were quartered for the night in churches and in the Capitol building. The next morning Governor Curtin reviewed the regiments from the Capitol steps. Then on moved the army—and Blythe—to Camp Scott at York.

General Negley took command of both the Twelfth and Thirteenth Regiments. The Thirteenth was sent to Camp Brady at Chambersburg, where it joined other outfits. Next it went to Camp Riley, Maryland, and then to Camp Hitchcock in Berkeley County, Virginia. It crossed the Potomac at Williamsport, Maryland, with General Patterson's men, then recrossed and took up quarters at Camp Niles until July 4. Blythe was with them. At Camp Niles occurred an incident that must have delighted Blythe. The troops had been bitter about the ragged outfits issued them. Finally a consignment of new drawers arrived. When a visiting dignitary, a Mr. Schwartzwelder, asked to have the troops pass in review, the Thirteenth Regiment distinguished itself by preferring to parade by in the newly-issued drawers rather than in their ragged pantaloons. Blythe did use Camp Niles as the setting for a painting which will be discussed later, but if he sketched the review, the sketch is lost.

On July 4 the troops recrossed the Potomac while guns of General Doubleday saluted Independence Day. They camped until July 15 and then marched to within twelve miles of Winchester. Then they went to Harper's Ferry, and there crossed the Potomac a fourth time. Small wonder that later Blythe painted troops crossing the Potomac—one of his best pictures.

The troops headed for Hagerstown, marching the twenty-two miles in nine hours. Trains carried them on to Chambersburg, Harrisburg, and ultimately to Pittsburgh, where they were mustered out on July 29, after three months' service. Most of the soldiers re-enlisted at once and made up the One Hundred Second Pennsylvania Regiment, which had a long and distinguished record. But Blythe, the convivial and popular camp follower, the welcome guest around campfires and at mess and wherever soldiers trade yarns and while away time, did not go with the regiment. "He was a welcome guest at any mess he fell in with in constant wandering around," wrote one of the regiment. "On a number of occasions he got in trouble, being arrested and placed under guard, his queer appearance and shabby dress, unkempt hair and beard, and apparently aimless action, exciting the suspicion of strangers." So ended Blythe's army experience.

Back in his bare little studio, Blythe began to paint from

his sketches, from memory, and from the tales of returning soldiers. He talked about another great panorama, one of camp scenes and battlefields, but either his energy or his ambition or his money failed. The panorama was never begun. Instead he painted, spasmodically, small canvases with Civil War subjects. His erratic temperament probably prevented him from becoming so great a war painter as Winslow Homer, and even another Pittsburgh painter, John Donaghy, a young captain in the Twelfth Regiment.

Much that Blythe did these last four years of his life—aside from painting—is not known. He may have gone for awhile to the East Liverpool farm; his mother was nearing eighty and his brother Andrew had enlisted in the Union Army. He may have been busy in war work at Pittsburgh, which had become an arsenal of importance. He may have been active in political affairs; some of his poems and paintings show his deep interest in politics. It is certain he painted few pictures. Yet some he did paint are among his best.

One of his lesser Civil War paintings shows a soldier, weighted by a knapsack on his back, standing by a farmhouse well while a woman pours a dipperful of water into his flask. Age and neglect have dimmed much of the color; the pitched roof of the house, the broken fence at the right, the yard and the well, and even the woman's red dress are almost lost in the darkened browns.

And *Soldier Putting on Socks* has little distinction. A Union soldier in a red blouse sits by a stream tugging at his socks. Parts of his blue uniform and his knapsack and other equipment are on the grass by him. Near, on the bank, lie the ace of spades and a torn ace of clubs. Remnants of a recent card game or symbols of deeper significance? One must draw his own conclusions. The words "Camp Niles June 1, 1861," carved on a tree make clear the place and time. There are in the painting few of the qualities which give some of Blythe's Civil War work distinction. Its brown and sombre greens have little richness, nor does the soldier have individuality. The painting lacks the distinction of *Libby Prison* and *General Doubleday.*

Union Troops Entraining shows the Pennsylvania Station in 1861. Troops are leaving for camp. There are three central figures—a young soldier carrying a rifle, his mother clinging to his hand, and his old father standing by stoically. All about the station and far down the street the crowds mill about between the row of flag-draped buildings on the right and the line of railroad cars on the left. A few stand, unemotional. Some wave wildly. Soldiers look out of the car windows. Last-minute recruits rush to board the train. The painting catches the tension, the confusion, the patriotic fervor, yet it has simplicity and restraint. Blythe often clutters his paintings with details. In this one he masses and omits. It avoids the weakness of so many genre paintings—the overminute, the trivia, which divert from the theme by leaving little to be imagined.

In the small *Recruits Wanted* Blythe's sense of humor is like that in his prewar genre paintings. A young man in Blythe's favorite reddish-brown and orange stares at a recruiting poster tacked against a building. Large lettering on it tells: "A FEW *SOBER MEN* WANTED TO FILL UP . . . The point may be broadly stated, but the rough and casual brush strokes give softness and warmth to the painting; the slouched figure has something of the quality of a Winslow Homer fisherman; the subdued browns, the deep red of bricks on the ground, the slate gray of a distant mill roof are a pleasing color harmony.

Recruiting is the subject of *The Bounty Jumper.* The humor here is sharpened into more than amusement. The jumper wears brown trousers, blue shirt, red scarf. He stands reading from an enlistment poster on the wall of a warehouse:

To ARMS
When enlist $2
Pay in advance $13
Government bounty $25

Able-bodied men
Board — transportation
And a good time generally

What the man plans is clear—to sign up, get the bounty offered, desert, re-enlist, collect again, and repeat as often as he dares. Blythe makes no attempt at moralizing or satire. *The Bounty Jumper* reports without comment. Blythe is seldom crusader, reformer, or even a caricaturist with moral purpose. The painting is among Blythe's better Civil War work. It shows, for one thing, that he could paint the human figure in other than distorted poses. The man is drawn with a feeling for anatomical structure; it is again the mastery over form that suggests *The Shoremen.*

Much less distinguished is *The Story of the Battle.* Three persons are sitting on the porch of a frame home—probably mother, father, and daughter—listening to the son who, a little to the left of them, seems by his gestures to be describing the battle in which he lost a leg. The figures stand out rather sharply against the gray wall of the house. The background is tones of gray, touched here and there by other colors, as in the rain barrel and the pump and the green vines climbing to the porch roof. If Blythe meant only to catch a simple picture, he has succeeded; if he meant to dramatize a tragedy of war, he has failed.

The Story of the Battle merely sets a tableau. *Libby Prison* has power and drama. Perhaps the stories told by returning soldiers and the dramatic battle scenes drawn by Hillen, Crane, Becker, Forbes, Newton, Lawson, Wavill, and Nast in *Frank Leslie's Illustrated Magazine* and in the first and second numbers of *Harper's Pictorial History of the War*, April, 1863, roused Blythe. At the same time, too, a lithograph by Schuchman of C. E. McKenn's painting of the One Hundred Twenty-Third, One Hundred Thirty-First, and One Hundred Thirty-Fifth Pennsylvania Regiments in action was being exhibited in Pittsburgh and stirred much interest. At any rate, in 1863, whatever prompted him, Blythe painted one of his greatest Civil War pictures, *Libby Prison*.

Libby Prison in Richmond had been a big brick tobacco warehouse. In Civil War days it was a prison, with at times as many as 1,200 Union troops crowded into its dark bareness. The grim accounts by escaped prisoners made it one of the most notorious prisons of the war.

The painting is packed with details, yet the composition hangs together admirably. Blythe got this unity by skillful arrangement of lights and darks, colors and shadows. Each group stands out clearly—the card players, the chess players, the young man in solitary confinement, the chaplain—yet all are well-knit parts of the whole. The composition leads one from group to group, and back into the dark recesses and murky corners of the canvas. The grime and chill, the damp and mustiness are masterfully suggested. Blythe's color scheme is rich browns with dashes of deep red and dark green. Yet the coloring holds in its sombreness and gloom the grimness of the prison and the melancholy of its prisoners. The stone stairway leading to a trap door faintly visible in the dim shadows calls to mind Rembrandt, and there is, too, in the whole something of the chilling horror of Hogarth's *Bedlam*. Here is far more than anecdote or illustration; here is the depth and power of a high and significant work of art.

Two landscapes have the high quality of *Libby Prison.* Though one of these is unsigned, there is good reason to believe it is Blythe's. It shows the march of "Fighting Joe" Hooker's men up Lookout Mountain in late November, 1863. The column of troops winds up the steep slopes, past a gnarled tree draped with moss, along the rugged ledges, by rocks and jagged boulders. At the left, the valley is a pearly mist. The distant ranges are faint outlines of gray in the haze of low clouds. Two bright flags flash color in the blue line of marching men.

Blythe was not, of course, at Lookout Mountain. Details he got from newspaper accounts and soldiers, and, perhaps, from the sketches of Homer and Nast. The tree with Spanish moss is clumsily drawn, as if from Blythe's vague recollection of moss seen in the West Indies. On the other hand, the mountains are real; Blythe knew his mountains. This painting may, in idea and style and type of theme, give a hint of what the destroyed panorama was like.

On June 6, 1863, because of Lee's steady advance north, Pittsburgh organized a Committee for Home Defense. About 16,000 persons—railroad workers, mill laborers, prominent businessmen, even students from the colleges and the university, and probably Blythe—went to work throwing up redoubts and building batteries along the bluffs from the West End to Beck's Run, from Soho over Herron Hill and Bloomfield and Stanton Heights to the Allegheny River opposite Sharpsburg, and from old Uniondale Cemetery to Troy Hill. These defenses were never used. Gettysburg stopped Lee's advance, and the capture of the last of Morgan's raiders near New Lisbon ended all rumors of invasion. The city settled back into its usual ways. Blythe did not. In this exciting summer Blythe painted one of his most unusual and mature paintings, *General Doubleday Crossing the Potomac.* Blythe had been with the Thirteenth Regiment when it crossed the Potomac the four times. The sight of Patterson and Doubleday's men winding over green Maryland hills was firm and clear to Blythe. When, on June 8, 1863, the important news reached Pittsburgh that Doubleday had crossed a shallow turn in the Potomac on his march to Gettysburg, Blythe's own experience seems to have come back to him vividly, and he recorded his memory of lines of men in blue winding down the valley to the river and curving up over the hazy slopes that fade in the mistiness of the foothills. Again Blythe is more than illustrator, cartoonist, or maker of tableaux. He is a landscape painter sensitive to light and air and space. Many consider the *Doubleday* his masterpiece, though it is not typical of him either in style or substance or color. One great value, other than its own charm and loveliness, is that it demonstrates Blythe's breadth of interests, his versatility as a painter, and his extraordinary talent that was especially extraordinary because it was self-developed.

It is true that Blythe continued to paint some pictures the last year and a half of his life but the *Doubleday* is a high point in his art; his last paintings do not have the qualities and values of the great landscape. These last paintings are interesting for the insight they give into Blythe's interests and personality. They show Blythe the man rather more than Blythe the artist.

After the *General Doubleday,* Blythe painted in the next year and a half other Civil War pictures, two still lifes—the only ones he ever painted—and a self-portrait. Compared with many of his earlier paintings these have little importance as works of art, but they are extremely interesting for the glimpse they give of Blythe's political interests, his concern with national affairs and his interpretation of them, and something, perhaps, of his philosophy of life. Three paintings—*President*

Lincoln Writing the Proclamation of Freedom January 1, 1863; Lincoln Slaying the Dragon of the Confederacy (or Rebellion); The Blair Family—show Blythe's sharp understanding of Civil War issues. The *Proclamation* shows Lincoln sitting beneath a copy of the Presidential oath, in an attic room in the White House, writing the Emancipation Proclamation, which rests on his knee along with a Bible and the Constitution. Scattered around are symbols of the conflicting issues of the time, and their cluttered arrangement suggests the disunity of the nation: a key and the insignia of the Masons and of the Odd Fellows and of the Christian Church. A scales of justice is in the shadows. A bust of Jefferson Davis hangs from a corner of a cabinet—by the neck! A bust of Andrew Jackson looks down austerely from the mantelpiece. Piled here and there are documents having on them the names of national figures: George D. Prentice, editor of the *Louisville Journal,* a staunch supporter of the Union; Wendell Phillips, the orator—a firm abolitionist; John Buchanan Floyd, President Buchanan's secretary of war but during the Civil War a brigadier general in the Confederate Army. These probably are meant to suggest the pressures brought on Lincoln from many sides. The painting, itself, no longer exists, but a lithograph of it was printed in color by Ehrgott, Forbriger and Company of Cincinnati, and published by M. Depuy of Pittsburgh sometime in 1864.

It is possible that Blythe painted this to set the Northern interpretation of Lincoln's act against that in a bitter picture called *Emancipation Proclamation,* by a Southerner, Adalbert J. Volck. Volck's picture William Murrell describes in this way:

His (Lincoln's table) is supported by legs carved at the top into negroes' heads with ram's horns, and at the base into cloven hoofs. The devil holds the ink well, a snake's head writhes from the window hangings, a statuette symbolic of the United States is used as a hatrack, and pictures on the wall show a massacre by negroes in Santo Domingo . . . Surrounded by these inspiring objects and symbols, with one foot resting on a volume labeled "Constitution of the United States," Lincoln is wrestling with his message.

Lincoln Crushing the Dragon of Rebellion was painted in 1862. In it Lincoln is shown with a club lashing at a dragon representing the Confederacy. The dragon's tail is wrapped around pillars supporting the Union and these are beginning to crack and totter. Lincoln is hindered in his efforts to destroy the dragon; he is chained to a stump and the chain is held also by an Irish character with a clay pipe in his mouth, who probably stands for the Irish backbone of Tammany Hall, a center of opposition to Lincoln. The stump is surmounted by a liquor bottle and surrounded by a copy of the Constitution and a cracked liberty bell. Tammany Hall, itself, is shown beyond the stump, a porticoed building with the words "Tam . . . ny Hall"—a catface, probably the Tammany Tiger, is in the center—lettered across the lintel stone. Two figures stand in the doorway, possibly Horatio Seymour, governor of New York and Democratic leader of the opposition, and Fernando Wood, Tammany boss and mayor of New York City. The distant background is much like that in *The Blair Family*—a faint glow of smoke and fire and a sketchy outline of gallows and ruined structures. Again, Blythe's defense of Lincoln is clear; his indictment of the foes of Lincoln within the Northern ranks is sharp. The method is the same cartoon-like style of the *Emancipation*—lettering, symbols, caricatured figures, all arranged and drawn to report the issues involved.

The Blair Family follows much the same pattern. Blythe's interest in the Blair family can be traced back to February 22, 1856, when the Republican Convention, presided over by Francis Preston Blair, met in Lafayette Hall in Pittsburgh.

Some of the seeds of this convention had been sown in David C. Herbst's grocery store on the corner of Third Street and Cherry Alley, not far from Blythe's studio. In the store, men of all shades of political thinking gathered to plan a new party. Undoubtedly Blythe joined the discussions. It was a great day in Pittsburgh, in February, 1856, when delegates began assembling at the Monongahela House to organize the new party, so often discussed around the flour barrels and pickle kegs in Herbst's grocery. Blythe and his friends probably stood with the crowd about the entrance to the Monongahela House or ventured into its ornate lobby that rose four stories to the roof. Among the delegates were important men like Preston King of New York, Kingsley Bingham of Michigan, Senator Zacharish Chandler, John F. Porter of Wisconsin, Oliver P. Morton of Indiana, Horace Greeley, and perhaps most distinguished of all, Francis P. Blair of Maryland, former editor of the powerful Democratic *Washington Globe*, a supporter of Andrew Jackson, and soon to be adviser of President Lincoln. During the convention sessions, the large, rectangular, flag-draped hall was crowded as delegates debated "Resistance to the existence of slavery in any territory in the United States!" "Support for the free-soil men of Kansas!" "Admission of Kansas as a free state!" Francis P. Blair, as presiding officer, dominated the convention as he did the following June when the first Republican National Convention was held at Philadelphia to nominate for the Presidency, John C. Fremont.

After the election of Lincoln, in 1860, the Blair dynasty grew in power. One son, Montgomery Blair, a West Point graduate, became Lincoln's postmaster general, and a second son, Francis Jr., became a congressman from Missouri and later a general in the Union Army. At this point their activities can be picked up in Blythe's painting. Montgomery and Frank are painted beside a column of Blair House in Lafayette Square, Washington. Frank holds a dagger, probably intended for General Fremont, who stands a little distance from them. The relationship between Fremont and the Blairs dated back to the marriage of Fremont to Jessie Hart Benton, a daughter of Thomas Hart Benton, who was a close friend of the Francis Blairs. For a time the friendship between Fremont and the Blairs was strong: the Blairs supported the nomination of Fremont for the Presidency in June, 1856, at the Republican Convention in Philadelphia; they used their influence to have Fremont commissioned a major general. But, soon after, when he was sent to take command of the St. Louis area it was clear that the state of Missouri was not big enough to hold both Fremont and Frank Blair, Jr. Relations grew even more strained when an intimate friend of Blair's, General Nathaniel Lyon, whose name is painted on the column in the picture, was killed at Wilson's Creek through Fremont's failure to reinforce his position. Although this widened the rift, the decisive break came when Fremont issued a drastic proclamation of emancipation, which went far beyond the law enacted by Congress in July, 1861. By this highhanded action, Fremont was sure he could rid Missouri of rebels and settle the disturbing issues once and for all. He proclaimed martial law because of disturbances that followed the battle of Wilson's Creek; all persons found with arms inside the lines of occupation were to be shot; property belonging to those aiding the enemy was to be confiscated and their slaves freed. Fremont's proclamation provoked such a boiling in the already bubbling Missouri cauldron that Frank Blair, then a colonel in the Army, was much alarmed. He tried to counteract the order, but the upshot was the jailing of Blair for insubordination. Montgomery Blair sharply protested the arrest and had enough influence with Lincoln to get his brother released and ultimately to force a rescinding of Fremont's order. Lincoln wrote Fremont on September 2, 1861, that he disapproved the proclamation and requested Fremont to modify his orders. Fremont refused, and the President, himself, was compelled to modify the proclamation, September 11, 1861. In Blythe's picture, Fremont's order has been thrown on the ground. Blythe has interpreted the issue by representing the Blairs as conspiring to discredit Fremont by using the proclamation as a pretext.

Here and there in the picture are some names that need identification if Blythe's meaning is to be clear. The Mulligan on the column in the center is Billy Mulligan, one of Fremont's court of ruffians and soldiers of fortune, who proved so obnoxious to the conservative and aristocratic Blairs. "Fremont has authorized that notorious ruffian and felon Billy Mulligan to raise a number of his own class of ruffians in the City of New York and bring them out here . . . . I want you to stop this scheme . . . . " wrote Frank to Montgomery.

Greeley's hat with three leading newspapers thrust into its crown probably represents the chief source of propaganda for other editors and papers. The "Simon" on the brief case in the corner may stand for Simon Cameron and his fiddle-faddle policies.

The byplay of two little negroes in the foreground is interesting. Fremont's negro guards some baggage of the General and his wife. He thumbs his nose at Blair's negro. Blair's negro boy is asking—Blythe has written his question on a paper the boy holds—how it is that folks over there, in Missouri, are getting "modified," that is, reprieved from Fremont's sweeping proclamation so popular in the north among the abolitionists.

Blair's sympathies, however, are not entirely clear. Frank Blair with his dagger seems to be characterized as a conspirator. Blythe probably was an abolitionist—his letters to Hugh Gorley on political issues suggest this—and he may have supported Fremont's stringent policies and resented interference which brought about a modification of Fremont's policies. Yet the painting is free from violent prejudice; it is more pictorial reporting than a caustic caricature. In this, it is like most political cartoons of the time. Generally, even in the work of Charles, Akin, Clay, Johnston, and Nast, there is no rancor or venom, and the extreme exaggeration of European cartoonists, so effective in whipping up public opinion, is missing. By contrast with European cartoons, most American cartoons are mild. Blythe's is no exception.

Among Blythe's Civil War paintings are two little pictures which deserve brief mention, though they have not the artistic value of the *Doubleday* and the *Libby Prison* or the political interest of the *Emancipation* and the *Blair.* One is called *Meat for the Army* and the other *Army Mules.* The first has a brown and white cow grazing contentedly though she is *Meat for the Army!* In the second, two mules tethered to a tree, are staring about in lazy indifference. Since Blythe as a boy lived on a farm, it is not surprising that when he chose, he painted animals with almost the masterful draughtsmanship and something of the realism of Paul Potter.

Finally, there are two Civil War paintings that cannot be found. *The East Liverpool Mercury* of August 22, 1861, says, "Blythe has given us another one of his war pictures, equally racy and full of humor as anything that has yet come from his easel . . . . it represents a scene at Camp Scott, York, Pa." The picture evidently was painted either at York while Blythe was with the Thirteenth Regiment or soon after the Regiment was mustered out in Pittsburgh, in July, 1861. The phrase "another one of his war pictures" seems to show there must have been at least one other painted before the *Camp*

Scott. The Pittsburgh Gazette bears out that there was a painting of Camp Scott. Blythe, it prints, painted a scene "in company quarters in the fair grounds at York, Pa. in which Col. Rowley, Capt. J. Heron Foster, Capt. Gallagher, and other officers appear prominently. The picture is in the possession of Capt. M. K. Moorhead, Quartermaster of the Old Thirteenth." That is the last heard of the painting. The same article says a large painting was on exhibition in Fifth Avenue in the fall of 1861 showing Patterson's divisions crossing the Potomac into Virginia just before the battle of Bull Run. It is highly credible that this was Blythe's, since we know that he had seen four crossings of the Potomac in May and June, one of them by Patterson's Army. He could have reconstructed easily the scene then fresh in his memory. If the painting is ever found it will be interesting to compare it with the *Doubleday* landscape.

There are no other Blythe Civil War paintings as far as we know. Although his war paintings are few in number, they are generally of real quality. Had he painted no others than *Libby Prison* and the *Doubleday,* with their artistic merit, or *The Blair Family* and the *Emancipation,* with their political interest, Blythe would be among the important painters of the Civil War.

Besides the relatively few Civil War paintings that Blythe has left, there is one small record that should be included in discussing Blythe's life because it shows the tender affection he had for his family. His thoughts were with them constantly. In spite of his wanderings his affection never cooled.

Pencilled in a peculiar style like unjoined print rather than script, "i's" scrupulously dotted and "t's" carefully crossed, erasures and blots neatly avoided, is a letter written August 3, 1864, to his brother Andrew in the Union Army.

Dear Brother—We are just gathering in the details of your demonstration on Petersburg. It was surely a bold stroke; and although we are sorry it failed, so far as a victory was concerned, yet we (I mean the people) don't by any means count it a defeat. It proved at least three things—viz., strategy, strength, and courage. I hope you took part in it, and came out safe. What effect such stupendous demonstrations may readily have on men I can't say, but I think such a scene worth almost a life.

We have had another "big scene," owing to a rebel raid, not however, in force, across the "border." There is much dissatisfaction on account of the bungling of those, whoever they may be, who have charge of our border lines in this state and Maryland.

We have had some fine rains—hope they extended to your quarters, as rain will likely be your most welcome visitor these "warrum" days.

I profess to be somewhat schooled to the obstacles against which you run when you placed yourself under a knapsack, and imagination has kept me by your side, so to speak, ever since you left home. I think I know what you have suffered, but my dear brother, do your duty and never let it be said by "traitors" that your time given to your country changed you from a loyal citizen to a "copperhead," as some "sympathizers" say to our men. I hope Providence will spare you to return to blister our traitor-tongues that utter such against you.

I would like to hear from you, just now, to know your luck, as well as opinion on things generally.

Hoping everything for you, I am,

affectionately,

D. G. Blythe

Chapter Seven

SELF-PORTRAITS—STILL LIFE
DEATH—LOST PAINTINGS

IN ADDITION to the self-portrait in *Art Versus Law* Blythe has left only three likenesses of himself. One is a small—5″ × 8″—black and white sketch which shows him as tall, lanky, Lincolnesque, leaning on a fence post. He wears a tall silk hat, a coat, narrow-bottom trousers; a rather well-dressed figure except for his boots, one of which seems to be toeless! The face is bearded and stern, but sensitive and intelligent. With a minimum of lines Blythe has suggested character and personality. Judged by all descriptions of Blythe from those who knew him, this sketch seems to be an excellent likeness.

This is confirmed by his only preserved water color. In it he painted Isaac Broome and himself, early in 1865, standing before the doorway of J. J. Gillespie's where the two spent many hours. It is a much more polished self-portrait than the sketch; it is painted with great care. Blythe and Broome are very serious, dignified gentlemen. The background—Gillespie's large window with pictures and busts in it and part of the entrance to the bank next door—is merely suggested; the details give the illusion of reality without detracting from the two figures who dominate the picture. Aside from its being a good painting, it has two unusually interesting features. A greenish Washington two-cent postage stamp has been pasted on the wall of the bank beside the doorway and above a postal savings sign (a very modern bit of realism), probably by Blythe according to the present firm of Gillespie's, the painting's owner. And at the bottom of the painting, near an easel on which Blythe has signed his name, has been scrawled, perhaps by J. J. Gillespie, "Blythe and Isaac Broome, separated May 15, 1865" [the date of Blythe's death]. The painting has high quality. The soft gray tones, the modelling of the black clothes of Broome and Blythe, and the sketchy but suggestive outlines of the background are well done. One wonders that Blythe did not use water color more. Perhaps he did, and perhaps the paintings are lost through time and neglect.

A third self-portrait was scratched on a scrap of sandpaper. The familiar bearded face can barely be made out. It is impossible to determine when this was done, or where. The sketch is now in East Liverpool. It was probably drawn on one of Blythe's visits home.

Blythe has not put himself in any of his paintings, as Jan Steen and many other European painters have done; unless a bearded figure near a window in *Libby Prison,* thought by some to resemble Blythe, is the exception. He might naturally have fancied making himself a witness of many ludicrous incidents he painted, but such seems not to be actually so.

Blythe painted only two still lifes. They were done in March, 1864, only two months before his death. At that time, for $25 apiece, Blythe painted two 8″ × 12″ companion pictures for C. H. Wolff: *Old Age* and *Youth. Youth* has a

LIBBY PRISON (M. and M. Karolik Collection, Museum of Fine Arts, Boston, Mass.)

GENERAL DOUBLEDAY CROSSING THE POTOMAC
(National Museum of Baseball, Cooperstown, N. Y.)

blue-green paper-backed ABC book, a penknife, marbles, a ball, two candy sticks, a spoon, a slice of cake, and a firecracker, all tumbled on a table, as a little boy might empty them from his pockets. But, in addition, there is on the table an hourglass, nearly full; many rich years lie ahead for this boy. Within the dreamy haze of the background is outlined the symbol of his ambitions: the dome of the Capitol. In the companion piece, the hourglass is almost empty, the candle almost burned down to the holder. Walking stick and eyeglasses rest on the Holy Bible beside a yellowed letter. The background is a blur: old age has been reached; life has nearly run its course; a boy's fancies and ambitions are gone, unrealized.

The paintings are small and simple but they prove that Blythe, when he chose, could do correct drawing and model objects subtly. He was a craftsman when he wished to be. These are probably his last pictures. They may symbolize Blythe's own life as he saw it: a boyhood filled with zest, enthusiasm, ambition, hope; resignation to the end of life, a life commonplace and undistinguished, and soon to end. In 1865, his life probably did seem commonplace to his contemporaries and even to him, if he weighed the little he had done and gained. But time has a way of sifting the rare from the commonplace. Soon to end? That much was true. The sands of the hourglass had almost run, the candle had almost burned to the base. Before two months would pass, Blythe's career would end.

In April, after he painted *Old Age* and *Youth,* Blythe scratched a final poem, published in *The American Standard.* It is an especially interesting poem because it is moonlight and love and music, and in its last lines holds the touch of grotesque humor that is in most of his work and that stayed with him in his living.

A Night Scene

The cold round moon looked brightly down
And ever as she looked she threw
Upon an arbor, trail'd with green,
Just such a silver-sheeted sheen
As cold round moons can only do.

Silence stood tiptoe, listening,
Whilst floating through the mid-night air—
Some without, and some with wings—
Ten thousand immaterial things
Came and went, the Lord knows where.

Music—with its melting charms—
From some far-distant "window-pane"
To nature's sweet, sad, soothing spell
Added something as it fell,
Mingling its mellowed strain.

Scattered flakes of deepest shadow,
Like fun'ral trappings on the ground—
Side by side, with moonlit patches—
Lay, revealing spectral snatches—
Of a thousand things around.

And there among a thousand other
Things, the light and shade revealed
Sat a maiden and her lover—
He beside—the moon above her—
Peeping through their viny cover—
Wondering why they didn't smother,
Sitting squeezed up to each other
Like toes jammed into high-heeled
Boots,
April, 1865.

On the morning of May 14, 1865, one of the Flemming brothers, who owned a drugstore at 60 Wood Street where Blythe bought his paints, stopped as he often did to pass a word or two with Blythe. When he went into the room, he found Blythe lying on the floor, near death. He called aid, and Blythe was taken to Passavant Hospital nearby. Blythe died the next day. At fifty Blythe's brief, erratic, vivid career was over.

The Pittsburgh Evening Chronicle of May 15, 1865, carried the following notice:

David Blythe Esq., a well known artist of this city, is now lying dangerously ill. We are unable to learn the nature of his disease but from circumstances brought to our knowledge we are led to believe his sickness was superinduced by want of the necessities of life. Mr. Blythe had painted many fine pictures—generally of a comic character—among them most prominent the "Horse Market" and the "Southern Confederacy." He also has written a number of poems, songs, etc. He was this morning taken to Passavant Hospital. Since writing the above we have learned that Mr. Blythe is dead. We shall give a more extended notice of him when opportunity affords.

The next day *The Pittsburgh Gazette* printed that Blythe died from "what was pronounced by the physicians to be of the nature of apoplexy."

His brother Andrew came at once to Pittsburgh. He took the body to the old Fifth Street Cemetery in East Liverpool. Years later, when this cemetery was closed, his remains were reburied in Spring Grove Cemetery, originally the God's Acre of the Blythe farm. Blythe rests with his family, on a slope overlooking the Ohio in the valley below. A small upright stone with the words "David G. Blythe, died May 15, 1865, Aged 50 years" marks the grave.

Many of Blythe's contemporaries felt affection for him, and some even realized the worth of his work. The morning after Blythe's death, *The Daily Post* of Tuesday, May 16, 1865, made this comment: "The deceased was of a singular turn of mind, but was possessed of an idea of the ludicrous in a rare degree, and had the ability to put it on canvas in an artistic manner."

On June 8, 1865, the same paper said that in honor of "... the late David Blythe, the peculiar local artist and Hogarth of Pittsburgh, friends were planning to erect a suitable testimonial over the grave of the lamented artist. James Dickinson of the theatre ... presided, and J. J. Gillespie who has done so much to encourage native talent, was elected chairman of the finance committee."

A week or so later, on Wednesday, June 21, *The Daily Post* announced that "in Gillespie's window, No. 86 Wood Street, a model for the monument to the lamented Blythe can be seen. It was designed by Isaac Broome of this city, and is what is technically known as a 'mud model.' It represents the artist seated ... on a four-sided pedestal, book in hand, in the act of making a preliminary drawing. The contour of the features and body are life-like and would at once be recognized by any friend of the singular but gifted artist. Upon the front of the pedestal appears the following inscription: 'erected by the friends of David G. Blythe in token of their admiration of his artistic genius A.D. 1865.'"

That the model was lifelike may well have been true, for Broome and Blythe were close friends and if anyone could reproduce Blythe's features and gestures in clay it would have been Isaac Broome. A small photograph of the model also seems to bear out the paper's statement, although to be sure, the model is a somewhat idealized figure of Blythe.

A box for contributions to the "testimonial" was placed in Charley Bear's tobacco shop on Wood Street, and other efforts were made to raise money. On Wednesday, July 12, *The Daily Post* printed this news item: "The friends and admirers of this native child of genius intend to give a grand entertainment at Masonic Hall, for the purpose of aiding the fund (of which J. J. Gillespie, Esq. is treasurer) to erect a testimonial to the lamented artist in the cemetery. Itinerants of the drama, resident professionals and amateurs, and musical celebrities have volunteered their assistance, and if citizens do not put in an appearance, they should." No further newspaper accounts can be found to tell the outcome of this; one fact is clear—the "testimonial" over Blythe's grave was never built.

Indeed, the evidence is strong that Blythe's friends, however sincere and well-meaning, soon forgot all about him—except for a few of his eccentricities. Even many of his paintings became scattered and lost; there is no way of estimating how many. The lost paintings fall into three groups: those which Blythe undoubtedly painted during the many months of his life of which we have no records; those of which we have descriptions but which are missing—either lost or destroyed; finally, those known to us today only by titles in catalogues of exhibits held years ago.

Of the second group, the *Coal Carrier* is typical. We know that such a painting was painted because we have fragmentary descriptions. It showed an old Frenchman who earned a living by hauling coal. Blythe painted him trudging up a bleak hill, with shovel and basket strapped to his back.

Another painting, a favorite in Blythe's time, and much sought after by collectors of Blythes, is the *Democratic Procession.* Political parades were common enough in Pittsburgh those days. Newspapers tell of many a one which wound up on the sand bar in the Monongahela for barbecues and beer. Blythe, an ardent Republican, seems in this picture to have delight in emphasizing ridiculous details of one parade. Leading it as chief marshal rides Robert Patterson, Esq. astride a fine white horse between whose feet darts a large hog. Next comes a wagon drawn by a decrepit old horse and filled with white-robed young ladies representing the thirteen original states. Behind this straggles a mob of shouting, heckling youngsters. The procession is passing along Fifth Avenue and nearing Wood Street. A saloon is on one corner, on another the Post Building. At one of its second-story windows, John Dunn, editor of the *Post,* and J. P. Barr, the owner, peer down from behind a row of whiskey bottles. Along the curb a crowd—many of the city's first citizens are shown—is watching the parade with great interest. The picture naturally raised a storm—praise from Republicans, whose politics let them enjoy this unflattering comment on the Democrats, and wrath from those whose dignity had been offended. The *Post,* of course, assailed it bitterly. Years later the painting hung in Newell's Bar on Fifth Avenue; and that is the last record we have of it.

Also missing is an early painting, *Deacon at Prayer.* In this a man kneels piously in prayer while a little boy holds up by the tail a screeching cat.

The Bum, Lemon Tom, Pay Your Toll, The County Commissioners' Office, and *The Card Party* to this day have escaped collectors of Blythes. Agnes Way's clippings give us descriptions of two of these: "One of Blythe's works, 'Whist Party in Judge Wilkins' Home' *(The Card Party)* has mysteriously disappeared. Carnegie Institute was accused of secreting the picture because it was supposed to show Andrew Carnegie playing cards. To the contrary, the Institute's Fine Arts Department has been scouring the country to find the painting." In spite of his eccentric and independent manner ("when called upon by the best people in town, he would scarcely deign to offer them a chair") Blythe was a welcome guest at the best homes. He had a charm, evidently, that endeared him to those in drawing room as well as tavern.

Another clipping from Agnes Way's Scrapbook reads: "The pioneer of painting in Pittsburgh, Blythe, is represented in this exhibition [probably the Public Library Exhibit of 1879] by one of his characteristic pictures. Defective in drawing, and working without care or finish, the humorous genius of the man enables him, by a few nonchalant strokes of his brush, to tell a story with graphic force, for which many a painstaking artist sighs in vain. In *Pay Your Toll* the grim face and resolute forefinger of the tollkeeper and the hesitating attitude of the passenger, whose reluctant hand is pursuing a penny through the dreary depths of his pantaloon pockets, portrays as clearly the subduing power of stern necessity." Tolls had become irksome to Pittsburghers. Dr. Leland Baldwin in *Pittsburgh: The Story of a City* quotes this jingle:

> "So long as our globe continues to roll,
> So long will our bridges expect to take toll."

These paintings may have been destroyed or may be buried under layers of dust in attic corners. Some may yet be found. *The County Commissioners' Office,* the *Democratic Procession,* and *The Card Party,* especially, would help in a complete judgment of Blythe's painting.

Of a number of paintings shown in the Public Library Exhibit of 1879 there are no descriptions. In this group are: *John Brown,* then owned by Rev. S. J. Travelli of Sewickley; *Higher Law* and *Foreign Loans,* owned by Capt. C. W. Batchelor; *Luxury,* owned by J. Painter and Sons; *The Schoolmaster,* owned by James Park, Jr.; *Corn Husking,* owned by a Dr. Shallenberger; *Slaying the Dragon,* owned by George R. Duncan; *Old Virginia Home,* owned by Joseph H. Davis (which may be the *Story of the Battle* now in the Duquesne Club Collection); *Calculating the Chances* and *The Painter,* owned by Alexander Nimick (the first may be the painting now known as *Prospecting*. The latter is described vaguely by Mr. Nimick as showing a painter at work before his easel with a donkey peering over his shoulder); *Room for Improvement,* owned by D. C. Holmes; a pencil sketch called *Sick Headache,* owned by John F. Marthens; and *Rustic Courtship,* owned by Mrs. Isaac Jones. Many of these may be known today by different titles.

Exhibited at the second Associated Artists' Show in 1860 and untraceable are these: *Hopeful Grandson,* lent by Dr. W. M. Wright, and *Egg Thief,* lent by James S. Craft. Two paintings shown in the 1914 Associated Artists' Show cannot be found: *Pap Beitler's Roadhouse,* lent by John F. Scott, Jr., and the *Slave Market,* lent by J. C. Thompson.

One of the first pictures Blythe painted after he came back to Pittsburgh in 1856 is lost, unless it is now known by another title. It was called *Young America,* a 22″ × 27″ canvas. Mr. C. H. Wolff bought it from Mr. Henry Miner of Pittsburgh in January, 1858, for $40, "including the frame."

From East Liverpool comes word that Blythe once painted a grocery store scene. It would be interesting to compare this painting with Alburtis D. O. Browere's *Mrs. MacCormick's General Store,* which strongly suggests Blythe's style.

Although Blythe's paintings, when displayed in Gillespie's windows, "were the talk of the town, and attracted such crowds that one could scarcely get along the street," he got little money for them. At the height of his popularity the *Gazette* of Saturday, June 16, 1864, printing the prices paid at an auction the night before, reported that Wall's *View of Juniata* brought $80, Broome's *Wounded Soldier* $20, a McClurg $80, a Hetzel $90, and Blythe's *Old Virginia Home* $30. When, in 1859, Blythe's delightful *Dry Goods and Notions* was bought by Mr. C. H. Wolff, Blythe was paid $35. George W. Hailman of Pittsburgh paid $35 for the *Post Office,* now in Carnegie Institute; this was the usual amount, according to Mr. Wolff, for a Blythe painting.

But these small prices probably satisfied Blythe. His wants, it seems, were few. He was little concerned about money. There are two legends which, because Blythe was Blythe, seem very credible. One is that he had a permanent drawing account at Gillespie's, where he left his paintings to be sold. Blythe is said to have used this account sparingly, never drawing out more than five dollars at a time. Another legend is that a prominent banker opened a substantial account for Blythe but that Blythe withdrew only one dollar. Blythe seems to have preferred to handle his finances in a way quite his own. With contempt for conventional currency, Blythe paid his debts with paintings. Many merchants or bankers were glad to foot the bill at cafes in exchange for Blythe's company. Blythe never forgot the indebtedness. He paid with a picture. So it has come about that many of Blythe's paintings have been found in the basement or attics of prosperous old Pittsburgh families, placed there, it is suggested, by wives who saw little humor or beauty in their racy wit. Some have just now, after years of dusty seclusion, become the center of art dealers' fancy. Many, unfortunately, were looked upon as trash and destroyed. A few have found their way to second-hand dealers, where more than one rebought for $10 or $15 has brought its lucky discoverer a hundred times what he paid. Such is the tale behind more than one Blythe painting in galleries and private collections.

Like Stephen Foster, his contemporary in Pittsburgh, David Blythe never in his lifetime had the recognition or the money his art should have brought him. Like Foster, he died penniless and for the most part overlooked. Blythe's paintings, like Foster's ballads, so full of the real spirit of the America he knew, so in tune with the ways of the age that they were accepted as commonplace, waited a century for the perspective of time to bring them just appreciation.

Because appreciation finally has come to David Blythe it seems right to examine the nature of it, and the justification for it. To estimate his painting and his position in American art is not easy. Much room is left for the dangerous pastime of speculation and imagination: many of his pictures are lost and few records remain to help make clear the emotions and ideas and occasions behind his paintings. One can, however, on the basis of the paintings and the facts which are available suggest the qualities and characteristics of Blythe's paintings and his place in the history of American painting.

Chapter Eight

CRITICAL ANALYSIS OF BLYTHE'S PAINTINGS

AS A BACKGROUND for a criticism of his work, it is interesting to bring together comments on Blythe and his paintings, some written by his contemporaries, some written soon after his death, and some written more recently by art historians and critics. They represent the appraisals most often made.

The Daily Post on Thursday, June 8, 1865, characterized Blythe this way: "... David Blythe, the peculiar local artist and Hogarth of Pittsburgh ... a singular, but gifted artist."

The Pittsburgh Evening Chronicle on March 11, 1864, commented: "We are glad to see that our friend Robitzer, whose sketch of the *Chronicle* newsboy attracted so much attention in Mr. Gillespie's window a short time since, has taken up the brush as a permanent business and now intends to devote his whole time to the profession. He is a most excellent portrait artist and has a dash of humor in him not inferior to Blythe."

The Pittsburgh and Allegheny Illustrated Review, 1889,

mentioned Blythe briefly: "One of the earliest artists of this city who is recognized and identified with the beginning of art in Pittsburgh, was Blythe, whose forte was humorous sketches. He was an original and competent artist, but his financial success was poor, and he was one day found dead in his studio."

In Agnes Way's Scrapbook is a clipping undated and unsigned: " . . . as I glance over them, I can hardly resist the impression that the captain (John Donaghy) has not a little of the genius of Blythe, who but for whiskey, might have made himself a name among the highest in the country, even among the artists of Europe . . . There is . . . a rougish wink in the boy's eyes which Blythe himself could hardly have beaten . . ."

The Pittsburgh Gazette, April 4, 1895, thirty years after Blythe's death gives this judgment of him: "Our eccentric artist painted a great many portraits, but never professed to make that . . . a specialty. He made a specialty of nothing, not even of business. He painted because it was his nature to do so, and apparently not for a livelihood . . . always a comparatively poor man. His landscape sketches displayed as much genius as . . . his character pictures. He never placed a commercial value upon his talent. While working in Pittsburgh his productions would be . . . found in Gillespie's windows, Wood Street. If he ran short of funds, which was a frequent occurrence, Blythe would go to Gillespie's for a dollar or perhaps a 'V,' but he would not accept more than was required for his immediate needs."

The Gazette in 1895 wishing, it seems, to revive interest in Blythe asked for information from those who remembered him. Many of the statements, rising out of the fog of dim memories are inaccurate, as later has been proved, but they all emphasize his eccentricities, his independence of character, his complete honesty, his passionate patriotism, his carelessness of dress, and his convivial nature. Many related some incident to confirm their statements. These may be found in the files of *The Gazette* of that year. Within the stream of comments runs a strong current of deep respect and affection for Blythe.

Martin B. Leisser wrote in *The Pittsburgh Gazette Times* on May 2, 1910: "David Blythe has a unique and interesting character . . . He had little or no academic training, but his natural ability for painting and drawing and a gift for pictorial conception . . . enabled him to fully satisfy, delight and entertain the observer of his work. Illustrative and storytelling subjects chiefly occupied his brush. Though his drawing and construction were faulty at times, and he could hardly have been called a strong draughtsman, yet there was always a genuine feeling evident in his coloring. He was a welcome guest at the homes of many of our leading citizens . . . and incidents connected with his visits would furnish subjects for pictorial illustration. . . . The home, streets, politics and army life furnished him with ample material that was always highly enjoyed by the picture loving public when displayed in the windows of our art stores."

Penelope Redd in *The Post* of July 29, 1923, wrote: "Pittsburgh was not lacking in the genre painter . . . In David Blythe Pittsburgh had an . . . original artist. He seemed to have a vein of fancy and appreciation of the comic that is Elizabethan rather than Victorian. He never seems to have been touched by the sentimentality of his day. Even his anecdote of the wounded soldier is interesting aesthetically [*Soldier Putting on Socks?*] rather than emotionally. The method of painting the figures is free from the meticulous. His other large painting . . . is a fanciful conception of an Elizabethan green with the business of a coach call [*Stage Coach?*]. Bits in this are piquant."

The exhibition of Blythe's paintings at Carnegie Institute in 1932 brought some interesting comments. In the *Pittsburgh Sun-Telegraph* of December 23, 1932, Penelope Redd wrote: " . . . lack of technical training which his friends lamented as an obstacle to the fulfillment of his career is in modern eyes one of his assets. [His work] free of the formula imposed by Dusseldorf or Rome, the painter's Paris-dises of that era . . . honestly American and Provincial. . . . genuinely sensitive artist who reflected the temper of his times always with humor and on occasions with gleams of absolute beauty." Harvey Gaul, writing about the same exhibition, says Blythe had a "quick eye for picturesque genius and possessed magnificent Hogarthian humor. America was ribald in those days, and uncouthness stuck out in every beaver hat. The miracle of Blythe is that he was self-taught."

In 1936 the Whitney Museum of American Art exhibited Blythe's work. *Time* caught the popular view of Blythe and printed on April 20, 1936: "Blythe . . . unkempt, red-whiskered, hard-drinking, and contemptuous of his popularity." Lloyd Goodrich, in writing the introduction to the catalogue of the Blythe-Beal Exhibit at the Whitney, sums up Blythe's work by saying: "His early portraits are marked by a woodenness and meagerness typical of the provincial limner. The portraits of the middle 1850's are more skillful with an ease of handling and romantic warmth of color that suggest Sully or some representative of the English portrait tradition." Of his genre Goodrich uses these phrases: "Love of the ridiculous . . . satirical appreciation of foibles of fashion and oddities of character; relish of the low comedy of drinking and vagabondage . . . racy art . . . delighting in squalor, knavery, and mischief of a frontier community." He adds: "Some of the spirit of a Brouwer or a Hogarth reappears . . . showing in the grotesque originality of his forms with its curiously knowing simplifications and distortions, in the wit that included only the essentials, and above all that strain of caricatural madness that is the work of the genuine satirist in every age and century."

Evelyn Abrahams writes in *Antiques,* May, 1935: " . . . he could paint an excellent portrait, much in the manner of Gilbert Stuart. . . . Like Hogarth and Daumier, Blythe saw people through eyes unobscured by any film of sentimentality or pretense. . . . where Hogarth and Daumier are caustic . . . Blythe sees only the ridiculousness of human self-importance."

Alan Burroughs in his *Limners and Likenesses* says " . . . it is a pity that this later, popular art was not founded on the work of other early American genre painters . . . David G. Blythe . . . or Mount . . . who could represent daily life with enough intensity to make it seem important. . . . Neither Bingham nor Mount could rival an obscure itinerant woodcarver and portraitist who, settling down in Pittsburgh in the middle of the century, turned suddenly on contemporary life a sophisticated, sardonic and twinkling eye. Born in 1815, David G. Blythe was evidently gifted with a temperament akin to Quidor's. But whereas Quidor retreated into literature for inspiration, Blythe went to the 'Post Office' . . . for action and watched the fight for letters at the General Delivery Window, or stopped to chuckle at 'Dry Goods and Notions.' Whatever his training may have been, he ended by painting roisterously in the combined styles of Ostade and Brouwer. His little boys are not cherubs, but sneak thieves, and his noble citizens are sly carpetbaggers.

"If it is strange that so little has been made until recently of the work of Bingham, and nothing of the work of Mount, it is stranger still that Blythe has remained practically unknown outside of Pittsburgh, since his genre has all the racy vigor that is lacking in the 'subartistic' productions of

Brown and the technical feats of Woodville and Wood."

The Art News on October 26, 1940, says of Blythe's *Horse-market:* "The acme of Blythe is satire, coarse and bitter as reflecting the bitterness of his own life after his wife's death . . . He paints with the mordant touch of Rowlandson while in the beautiful atmospheric background is the pearly touch of an English landscape master . . . Blythe, the Victorian version of Rowlandson . . . " The same magazine on April 18, 1936, describes Blythe's portraits "a pallid lot" but calls "'Union Troops Entraining' a . . . successful composition . . . (full of) . . . tonal contrasts . . . " and adds, "'Court Room Scene' . . . has bits of Daumier . . . "

So Blythe's name has been linked with Hogarth, Daumier, Rowlandson, with the seventeenth century Dutch and Flemish genre painters Ostade, Brouwer, Teniers, Steen, sometimes with Brueghel, and with his contemporary Americans Quidor, Mount, and Bingham. There is some justification for this; many characteristics of Blythe's work do suggest these painters and many details prompt comparisons. There are similarities in theme often, sometimes in purpose, occasionally in style. But Blythe is the disciple of no one, the exponent of no school. Most of the analogies rest merely on details, not on essentials—a head here, a figure there, an interior corner, a tone, a brush stroke, a modelled object. What Blythe has borrowed from prints, reproductions, and illustrations are accessories, trivialities. He went his way, not much "influenced" by others' paintings. He was no copyist; he was too independent by temperament and too individualistic by nature. Nor was he an eclectic; he was alive to the work and style of others but what he absorbed from them he created into his own purpose and adapted to his own talent. Comparison of Blythe with other painters makes an entertaining analysis, yet the comparisons touch mere superficialities.

PRESIDENT LINCOLN WRITING THE EMANCIPATION PROCLAMATION
(Harry Shaw Newman Gallery, New York.)

THE BLAIR FAMILY (George D. Thompson, Pittsburgh, Pa.)

Blythe as a Pittsburgh Hogarth is an especially interesting idea; there is a basis for coupling the two. Just as no one before or since Hogarth has so vividly mirrored London life of the eighteenth century as he has, so no one so vividly mirrored Pittsburgh life of the nineteenth century as Blythe. And there the analogy ends, for their purposes and their themes and their styles differ. Hogarth is a satirist and a moralist first—in his own words in *The Analysis of Beauty,* his paintings were "pictur'd morals." His paintings often have a brutality and a vulgarity rare in Blythe. Blythe is seldom the moralist or the satirist; where the moral point is made, it generally amuses rather than bites. Reform is in Hogarth; tolerance in Blythe. Ridicule is Hogarth's method; fun is Blythe's. Nor does one find in Blythe the elaborate settings common in Hogarth or Hogarth's sense of a stage setting and a striking dramatic moment consciously staged. In Hogarth these are pronounced. He referred to himself as an author rather than an artist. He declared, "My picture is my stage, and men and women my players, who by means of certain actions or gestures are to exhibit a dumb show." His backdrops are usually ornate, beautifully arranged and painted. They show a passion for architectural and ornamental detail and an emphasis on draughtsmanship that Blythe never used or seemed to want. In Hogarth one sees the characters arrested at one moment of a drama with a *before* and an *after.* He says he wishes "to give to his pictures all that an actor can on the stage." In Blythe the pictured activity has a vitality and a continuity that give it movement with a *before* and *after,* but it is not arrested action; it is action itself. They did have this in common: they painted vigorously and with keen insight the life they knew, catching not the superficial and transient but the frailties and vices found as readily in twentieth century London and Pittsburgh as in those cities of a century or two ago. But their purposes and their methods of interpretation were far different.

In some ways, Blythe shares a closer relationship with two later English genre painters, Rowlandson and Cruikshank. Rowlandson's pen and wash sketch, *The Exhibition "Staircase,"* for example, has in the fat figures tumbling down the stairway the rough free strokes and sweeping flow of movement often found in Blythe's work. The grotesque face of the gambler in the water color, *The Unlucky Gambler,* and the ugly grimaces of horses and riders in another water color, *Visit to an Old Acquaintance,* remind one of Blythe, though the mood of the pictures is more cynical. And when Rowlandson ventures into elaborate and detailed architectural backgrounds, he moves away from much resemblance to Blythe. So, too, the butler in Cruikshank's *The Runaway Knock* and the two terrified figures in *The Ghost* recall Blythe, but Blythe never attempted the highly detailed, carefully modelled backgrounds of *Grinaldi Shaved by a Girl* or *The Disturber Detected.* There is a suggestion of Blythe in Robert Dighton's water colors *Westminster Election* and *Men of War Board for the Fort of Pleasure* but the similarity is one of theme. The same difference is in Charles Bretherton's *A Trip to Scarborough* or Humphrey Repton's *The Pump Room at Bath.* The distorted, the grotesque, the humorous, the absurd, which are so often a part of genre are there, as in Blythe, but with these the relationship ends. However, Blythe is closer to Dighton and Repton in spirit than to many other English genre painters. He has almost nothing of the sentimentality of Wheatley or Morland, or the technical perfecting of Ford Madox Brown or Sir John Millais.

Comparison of Blythe with Daumier has some justification. Blythe's trial scenes, especially, have something of the satire and power of Daumier. Beyond this, the two have little in common. Blythe never painted the mob scenes with their political and social overtones. In some ways, Blythe seems closer to Chardin than to Daumier. Certainly there is a plastic vitality about some of Blythe's figures that recall Daumier, as, for example, the old man in *The Towman.* Yet again, the parallels apply only to details of the painting, not to the effect.

In style and substance and purpose Blythe's genre paintings most resemble the seventeenth century Dutch and Flemish painters. One will, of course, find little that is like Blythe in Vermeer, with his unusual interest in light and texture, or in DeHooch, with his delight in open doorways showing rooms beyond and tiled floors. Blythe shares Brueghel's interest in low society, but Brueghel, for all his interest in people, sometimes subordinates them to the landscape setting. In *Icarus Falling into the Sea,* for example, all of Icarus that is shown is a leg sticking up out of the water. The rest of the picture is sea and ships and land. Brueghel's religious subjects, though to be sure they are often religious only in title (in *Christ Carrying the Cross* the figure of Jesus is almost hidden in the crowd of Flemings), and his vividly colored village festivals have little that Blythe had. Steen sees life more widely than Blythe; he paints the attractive with the coarse, the pretty with the debauched, and does so with greater emphasis on realistic drawing and bright colors than on distorted figures and subdued tones. Ter Borch in *Boy Hunting Fleas* is like Blythe in subject but rather different in style. Terburg and Metsu's middle- and upper-class interiors are a little too placid for Blythe, with their quiet, dignified, graceful figures.

When one comes to Ostade and Brouwer and Teniers, the tie with Blythe in both theme and technique is much stronger and clearer. It has been said that these Dutch genre painters were painters first, illustrators second, moralists last if at all. This can be said, rather fairly, of Blythe. Often he was, instinctively, painter first. He delights in lights and shadows, and in composition. And if the anecdote is not subordinated to the composition, it is at least arranged with an eye to balance and harmony and accent. Ostade's *A Village Inn, Three Farmers Drinking, The Toothpuller, Interior of a Stable,* or Brouwer's *A Tavern Scene, An Operation, Two Carousers,* to name only a few of many, show the Blythe type of subject and style. They paint peasants—usually a small group—with distorted figures, ugly and often grotesque faces, going about their chores and pleasures. They paint with much the same soft, broad, often fuzzy brush strokes Blythe used. Their interiors show corners and recesses and jugs and kegs almost lost in a play of dimmed shadows and lights. They mass and simplify forms and objects. They eliminate almost all details. But except where Blythe consciously experimented in painting like Teniers his compositions and people are quite his own. Purpose and attitude are more important in relating Blythe to the Dutch and Flemish genre painters than are subject and style. Blythe, like these painters, was interested not in moralizing or satirizing but in mirroring, in recording, the life of the people he knew. Like the Dutch and Flemish he delighted in distortion, in exaggeration, but usually he did this because he was amused and wanted to paint the fun he saw. He saw people through tolerant, quizzical, keen eyes, and he chuckled at them rather than sneered. Their art—Blythe and the Low Country painters'—was a racy, homely, rugged, earthy, intensely human art, minus the dramatic, the elegant, the social consciousness, the brutal, the didactic. They painted in the spirit of men who were at home with their subjects and in sympathy with them. They gave their work a warmth and vitality and depth often lacking in genre work, an intimacy and humanity that cannot be had in the posed or the pretty.

In most ways Blythe seems closer to the Low Country genre

painters of the seventeenth century than to his contemporaries painting in America. Though he often is classed with George Caleb Bingham, William Sidney Mount, Eastman Johnson, John Quidor, and occasionally with Thomas Waterman Wood and Richard Caton Woodville, he is not much like them except that they all painted everyday scenes showing activities and interests of ordinary folk. Bingham's work was far more vividly colored, more illustrative, and more literally pictorial than Blythe's ever was, and often, as in *Order No. 11,* far more aimed at propaganda. Blythe's ties with Mount seem a little stronger. Mount, too, paints in the low, lustrous tones of the Dutch—in a kind of Jan Steen fashion—and his subjects are farmers, tavernkeepers, blacksmiths, and ragged schoolboys. But Mount is more a conscious craftsman than Blythe; one often feels that his interest is greater in his skillfully realistic, highly polished technique than in his subjects. Mount's figures all have a degree of personality, but there is little of the distortion and exaggeration that give Blythe's people so much life. Eastman Johnson seems quite far from Blythe because his pictures romanticize his negro slaves and New England farmers; Blythe rarely romanticizes or idealizes his subjects. To go on contrasting Blythe's work with other American genre painters—Wood, Woodville, John Ehninger, Thomas Hovenden, Edward Lamson Henry, William T. Ranney, John G. Brown, John F. Weir, and a score besides—would show many points that separate them from Blythe in spirit and style. At the risk of oversimplification by a generalization, American genre may be characterized as very literal, very illustrative, usually lacking in satire and brutality and vulgarity, frequently polished to such high lustre of technical finish that the pictures are often a little artificial, often romantic, often sentimental. Only a few of the painters equalled Blythe in robustness and individuality and gusto. Blythe paints with a vigor and ruggedness that is truer to American life. There is more of the tang of American life in Blythe's paintings, much as one finds it, for example, in the present-day work of Paul Cadmus, Jack Levine, and William Gropper.

Though it is worth doing, to compare Blythe's paintings with those of others, it is more important to find what, in itself, he, as Blythe, painted—the substance, the style, and the essence of his work.

The bulk of Blythe's work is genre. To be sure, some of his portraits have merit and the *Doubleday* landscape has real distinction, but genre is Blythe's most frequent, most sincere, and most perfect expression.

Genre in art has been defined in many ways. Most generally accepted is the rather broad definition that a genre painting is the record of everyday, commonplace activities—the pleasures, vices, and follies, the work, play, and amusements—of ordinary folk, painted in a relatively realistic, straightforward, pictorial style. People usually dominate genre pictures and are shown in human, homely, down-to-earth moments. Genre does not give the historical, the monumental, the allegorical, the idealized. How much subjective qualities—satiric, didactic, sentimental, romantic, or religious—should enter true genre has been a question for critics: but certainly in what is widely accepted as genre, the absurd, the pathetic, the exaggerated, the ironical, or the kindly play of humor is very likely to dominate. This is the genre Blythe painted.

The question comes up: Why are modern critics and collectors interested in Blythe, this painter of nineteenth century Pittsburgh? It must be admitted that he played small part in the development of American painting. In thirty years he painted, so far as we know, few pictures—only one hundred or so genre, one water color, several landscapes, a small number of portraits. He made no prints, no illustrations for books or periodicals, identified himself with no society or league, supported no art movement, taught no one, left no followers. And it must be granted he was a very uneven painter. That much he painted is below his talent can be laid, probably, to indifference, to carelessness, to his erratic temperament, but though they rise from his temperament rather than from lack of skill or limitation of power, his lapses into dullness and mediocrity cannot be denied. Yet his best paintings are of so high a quality that Blythe deserves attention and analysis. These best paintings have vitality and wit, humanity and truth. Blythe is a significant painter even though he painted few pictures, some inferior pictures, and had little influence on the art of his times.

The high quality in Blythe's genre rises from his selection of intensely human, earthy subjects, his mastery of a style—composition, color, modelling—especially suited to his subjects, and an unusual insight into his subjects. He knows what to paint. He can paint. He is sincere, vivid, often witty. He understands and sympathizes and has no malice or bitterness.

Much has already been said of his choice of subjects—tramps, hoodlums, housewives, merchants, and the like in their everyday activities. Blythe went into the market places, the public buildings, the hangouts, into the alleys, the street-corners, and the water fronts, and he recorded what he saw. This need not be repeated here. In analyzing Blythe's style—the techniques he had at his command—what may be said? Blythe is not an obvious stylist, yet he has a technique that gives his genre life and individuality. Composition is important to Blythe in spite of his preoccupation with narration—with action and personality. He manages a remarkable integration of forms and objects even in those canvases which are filled with people, with symbols, or with background details, as are a few of his interiors. Whether by instinct or plan, unity is there, got generally by the arrangement of his lights and darks and of his forms and objects, by the repetition of masses and color, and by the movement of lines and shapes. He usually gets balance through a pyramid arrangement of figures and of background details, but there is enough variety of forms and shapes to keep balance from seeming obvious. Though one never thinks of Blythe as primarily a craftsman, he seems to have had a high sense of structure and unity.

Blythe uses color well, though he limits his range. The mellow, sombre colors that fit so perfectly his subjects never degenerate into that "gravy of burnt umber" with which, says Homer Saint-Gaudens, many painters of his times soaked their canvases. "But where is the brown tree?" Sir George Beaumont asked Constable. Blythe's deep, warm colors have the luminosity and richness of the Dutch painters. Occasionally time has darkened his colors and sometimes bad cleaning has dulled them, but for the most part the original tones have remained clear and satisfying.

Any analysis of Blythe's style needs to comment on his drawing and modelling. The awkward poses, the bulging eyes, the bulbous heads, the distorted bodies are, no question, painted deliberately for effect. They are Blythe's way of getting humor, or, occasionally, mild satire into his pictures. On the other hand, *The Shoremen* and *The Bounty Jumper,* for example, show that Blythe when it suited his purpose was quite able to paint people realistically and accurately. Nor should the absence of elaborate architectural backgrounds or ornate furnishings be taken to mean that Blythe could not paint them. For one thing, they were not a part of the settings Blythe chose; taverns and markets were usually more to his taste than avenues and drawing rooms. His tramps and hoodlums congregated around warehouses and alleys, and a flick of a line or a sweep of the brush were enough for his purpose. In his still lifes, where perspective and modelling seemed important to him, he paints his objects with a feeling for their form and texture, but in his paintings where people dominate the scene, his drawing and modelling are rough and easy and loose. He is content to suggest rather than be photographic, and perhaps because of this his people seem caught in a flying but significant moment of reality as the eye rather than as the camera would catch them. They are not posed, not artificial. Blythe paints with economy; there is just enough of line and mass to capture what is vital; no more. The lines are simplified, the nonessentials dimmed, the emphasis is where it is needed. Important figures are strongly three-dimensional; they are flesh and blood. In his best genres, Blythe seems instinctively to have felt the second of sharpest effect. This he records with a dash of line and a blob of shadow that capture the spirit of what he sees.

Important as selection of subjects and mastery of technique are in the success of Blythe's genre, these are, after all, only the tools, the mechanics of his painting. The distinction, the brilliance of Blythe's work comes from the insight and truth his technique expresses. He brought to his genre paintings a personality peculiarly keyed to seeing much and understanding much of the life and the people he lived among, and an amazing gift for recording on canvas what he saw and felt. By recording with absolute sincerity, he gave to his paintings a mood and spirit that raised them above anecdotes and tableaux. Blythe never had the cramping passion for tight, sharply modelled, artificially posed, highlighted illustrations of much other American genre. He was concerned with what went on in the minds and hearts of his people—what personality and character lay beneath the folds and texture of their garments. He wanted not only the action of the moment but the meaning of the moment. He gave each figure individuality, breathed life into him, and then let him go his clumsy way, in all his most foolish and human acts, mirroring him humorously and sometimes even a little reprovingly. Blythe avoided insignificant and distracting details as scrupulously as he avoided being sentimental, idealistic, or romantic. People dominate Blythe's pictures—often grotesque, distorted, ugly—but people with a vitality and humanness about them that make them very real. And because people are Blythe's chief interest, his backgrounds, though often delightfully painted, are usually sketchy and vague. When details of background or foreground are necessary to the meaning of the picture, Blythe paints the objects or symbols boldly. So, throughout Blythe's genre there is honesty and directness; he does not bother to be complex, subtle, or obscure. And though his way of saying a thing is remarkable for its force and simplicity, the ideas and feelings behind the technical expression are most worth underlining in any analysis of his work. He approached his subjects with sincerity and warmth and humanity. He was able to be both spectator and actor in the life he painted; he could stand a little apart and sharply scrutinize men and women, but he painted them humanly—as one of them, just as foolish or ridiculous as they were. Perhaps this was why Blythe never could be bitterly satirical; he was painting his friends—and himself.

Blythe's art was so perfectly in harmony with his times that his contemporaries considered it almost commonplace. Paradoxically, it was so tuned to the life about him—and this was his real genius—that contemporaries hardly heard it. It was a little amusing, perhaps, but very ordinary, they thought. And in spite of the tremendous individuality which gave his art gusto and an added spark of brilliance that cannot be defined, he had when he painted best the great painter's universal understanding of what is basic in people, of what endures everywhere, always. In his day, his art spoke the language of high and of low society. It could be enjoyed by the most naive and the most sophisticated. There was laughter in it for the slow, wit in it for the clever, and truth for the philosophic. And this holds today. Blythe painted nineteenth century western America as it was in barrooms and post offices and Army prisons, on street corners and water fronts and Civil War battlefields; today only the costumes and the props would need to be changed to show America of the 1940's. *The Horsemarket* is pretty much Forbes Field, and *The Stage Coach* a Fifth Avenue streetcar.

In part, what makes Blythe's art last is its type of humor. It is the peculiarly American humor which has courage enough and imagination enough to laugh at the passing incidents of life (though never at the meaning) no matter how stark and grim and deeply melancholy they may be. This humor unites Blythe with Americans of many other times. Like Stephen Foster and Mark Twain, for instance, Blythe is lighthearted though he met and understood well the heavier hours of living. The art of Blythe shows laughter and dismay, anger and foolishness, vanity and cunning of real persons. Moments of great passion and intensity are not in Blythe's art—he does not try to show them. He does see, and paint, with a light but sure touch, the everyday bits of drama—the significant, though momentary, in the lives of the people he knew. His teacher was his eye, his master was his wit and his heart, his subject was life. Blythe's paintings are worth enjoyment and praise, for human nature is the essence of them.

PAINTINGS
BY DAVID G. BLYTHE

The following list of paintings is a relatively complete one; new paintings, however, are being discovered from time to time. The list of owners is a relatively accurate one; Blythe's paintings, however, are changing hands frequently, making an up-to-the-minute record almost impossible.

PORTRAITS

(Oil on canvas unless otherwise designated)

Annetta Bentley . . . . Mrs. Benjamin Ross,
(25″ × 30″) Monongahela, Pa.

Samuel Black Bentley . . . . Mrs. Benjamin Ross
(25″ × 30″)

Elizabeth Black . . . . Mrs. Benjamin Ross
(25″ × 30″)

Ross Black . . . . Mrs. Benjamin Ross
(25″ × 30″)

William Blakely . . . . Heber H. Blythe,
(6″ × 10″) pencil East Liverpool, O.

Blythe and Isaac Broome . . . . J. J. Gillespie,
(20″ × 24″) water color Pittsburgh, Pa.

John Blythe . . . . Heber H. Blythe,
(25″ × 22″) East Liverpool, O.

Susan Blythe . . . . Heber H. Blythe
(25″ × 22″)

Mrs. Cynthia Bradshaw . . . . H. B. Barth,
(28″ × 25″) East Liverpool, O.

Dr. John Coburn . . . . Mrs. Duvern Coburn,
(21″ × 27″) East Liverpool, O.

Mrs. John Coburn . . . . Mrs. Duvern Coburn
(21″ × 27″)

Thomas Coburn .... Miss Mary G. Irwin,
East Liverpool, O.

Mrs. Thomas Coburn .... Miss Mary G. Irwin

Joseph Croxall and Grandmother Mrs. Harry E. Troll,
(26″ × 21″) Youngstown, O.

Fanny .... Mrs. Duvern Coburn,
(21″ × 26″) East Liverpool, O.

John Fisher .... Sanford E. Fisher,
(24″ × 26″) East Liverpool, O.

Mrs. John Fisher .... Sanford E. Fisher
(24″ × 26″)

Silas Gault .... Butler Art Institute,
(27″ × 22″) Youngstown, O.

Eliza Gardner .... Mrs. Lawrence Thomas,
East Liverpool, O.

George S. Harker, Esq .... H. N. Harker,
(oval) East Liverpool, O.

Mrs. Ella Logan Hill .... H. B. Barth,
(20″ × 27″) East Liverpool, O.

John W. Irons .... Fayette Masonic Lodge,
(24″ × 20″) Uniontown, Pa.

Isaac Watt Knowles .... Miss Dorothy Downing,
(20″ × 27″) London, O.

Mrs. Cynthia Logan .... H. B. Barth,
(25″ × 21″) East Liverpool, O.

James Logan .... H. B. Barth
(25″ × 21″)

James MacDonald .... Butler Art Institute,
(27″ × 22″) Youngstown, O.

Julianne Cooke MacDonald .... Butler Art Institute
(27″ × 22″)

John James Cooke MacDonald .. Butler Art Institute
(27″ × 22″)

Kay Noble MacDonald .... Butler Art Institute
(27″ × 22″)

Margaretta MacDonald........Butler Art Institute
(27″ × 22″)

Martha Malvina MacDonald....Butler Art Institute
(27″ × 22″)

William P. Morris.............Historical Society,
(21″ × 26″) East Liverpool, O.

Charles B. Ogden.............Charles B. Ogden Estate,
(20″ × 27″) East Liverpool, O.

Rebecca Mary Patterson.......Miss Mary G. Irwin,
(oval) East Liverpool, O.

Mrs. Eliza Rigby..............Miss Nell Manly,
(22″ × 27″) East Liverpool, O.

Job Rigby...................Miss Nell Manly
(22″ × 27″)

Sarah Ann Rigby..............Mrs. Hazel R. Mast,
(22″ × 27″) East Liverpool, O.

Self-portrait.................Mrs. Duvern Coburn,
(6″ × 4″) pencil on sandpaper East Liverpool, O.

David C. Thompson...........George S. Thompson,
East Liverpool, O.

John Thompson...............Luna Thompson,
(21″ × 26″) East Liverpool, O.

John C. Thompson............Mrs. Charles Bailey,
(28″ × 20″) East Liverpool, O.

Mrs. William Thompson.......George C. Thompson,
(21″ × 27″) East Liverpool, O.

Josiah Thompson.............George C. Thompson
(21″ × 27″)

Mrs. Jeremiah Webber and Son. A. E. Webber,
(27″ × 23″) East Liverpool, O.

GENRE, CIVIL WAR, LANDSCAPE, STILL-LIFE PAINTINGS

Army Mules..................Harry O. Eichleay,
(11½″ × 14½″) Pittsburgh, Pa.

Art vs. Law (24½″ × 20″)	Brooklyn Museum
Blair Family (19½″ × 20″)	George D. Thompson, Pittsburgh, Pa.
Bobbie Burns in Auld Clay, Biggen (20″ × 24″)	Mrs. Franklin C. Irish, Pittsburgh, Pa.
The Bounty Jumper (11½″ × 14″)	Mrs. Alexander Nimick, Sewickley, Pa.
Boy and Watermelon (26″ × 24″)	W. H. Vodrey, East Liverpool, O.
Cobbler's Shop (17″ × 22″)	W. H. Vodrey
Corn Fed (22″ × 26″)	Duquesne Club, Pittsburgh, Pa.
Couple Praying and Companion Piece (10″ × 14″)	Mrs. R. Lucien Patton, Ligonier, Pa.
Court Room Scene (26″ × 21″)	Mrs. J. Insley Blair, Tuxedo Park, N. Y.
Don Quixote (19¼″ × 23¾″)	Harry Stone Collection, New York, N. Y.
Dry Goods and Notions (22″ × 27″)	Duquesne Club, Pittsburgh, Pa.
Fiddler (12″ × 9¼″)	Harry Shaw Newman Gallery, New York, N. Y.
The Fire Cracker (22″ × 27″)	Duquesne Club, Pittsburgh, Pa.
General Doubleday Crossing the Potomac (30¼″ × 40″)	National Baseball Museum, Cooperstown, N. Y.
Good Times (12″ × 9½″)	Harry Shaw Newman Gallery, New York, N. Y.
Gouty Fisherman (23″ × 28″)	Feragil, Inc., New York, N. Y.
Hard Times (12″ × 9½″)	Harry Shaw Newman Gallery, New York, N. Y.

Title	Owner
Harvesting (10″ × 14″)	Heber H. Blythe, East Liverpool, O.
The Hideout (22″ × 26½″)	W. H. Vodrey, East Liverpool, O.
The Hunter (14″ × 19″)	Duquesne Club, Pittsburgh, Pa.
Interior, Family Group (25″ × 32″)	Duquesne Club
January Bills (20¼″ × 24″)	Garvan Collection, Yale University
Land of Liberty (20″ × 24″)	George D. Thompson, Pittsburgh, Pa.
Lawyer's Dream (20½″ × 24″)	Charles A. Finley, Pittsburgh, Pa.
Libby Prison (24″ × 36″)	M. and M. Karolik Collection, Museum of Fine Arts, Boston, Mass.
Lincoln Slaying the Dragon of the Confederacy (18″ × 22″)	M. and M. Karolik Collection
Man Cutting a Melon (28″ × 18″)	Harry O. Eichleay, Pittsburgh, Pa.
Man Drinking (19½″ × 23½″)	Harry Stone Collection, New York, N. Y.
Man Eating in Field (10″ × 14″)	Heber H. Blythe, East Liverpool, O.
Man Putting on Boot	Donald Scully, Pittsburgh, Pa.
Meat for the Army (11½″ × 14½″)	Harry O. Eichleay, Pittsburgh, Pa.
Medieval Village (19″ × 25″)	Duquesne Club, Pittsburgh, Pa.
Mischief Maker (Reluctant Scholar) (26½″ × 21¼″)	Beverly Wyatt, Inc., Pittsburgh, Pa.
News Boys	Mrs. John H. Ricketson III, Pittsburgh, Pa.

Old Age .... Mrs. Paul C. Wolff,
(6″ × 10″) Pittsburgh, Pa.

Ole Cezer .... Mrs. John C. Dilworth,
(14″ × 16″) Pittsburgh, Pa.

On the Sly .... W. H. Vodrey,
(26″ × 21″) East Liverpool, O.

Pittsburgh Horse Market .... Mrs. R. Lucien Patton,
(26½″ × 36½″) Ligonier, Pa.

Pittsburgh Post Office .... M. and M. Karolik Collection,
(25″ × 30″) Museum of Fine Arts,
Boston, Mass.

Pittsburgh Piety .... Harry Shaw Newman Gallery,
(20″ × 24″) New York, N. Y.

Post Office .... Carnegie Institute,
(20″ × 24″) Pittsburgh, Pa.

Prospecting .... Mrs. Alexander Nimick,
(9″ × 12″) Sewickley, Pa.

Recruits Wanted .... Mrs. Alexander Nimick
(8½″ × 11″)

Return of the Prodigal .... Harry O. Eichleay,
(8″ × 12″) Pittsburgh, Pa.

The Runaway .... Duquesne Club,
(18″ × 24″) Pittsburgh, Pa.

Street Urchins .... Butler Art Institute,
(27″ × 22″) Youngstown, O.

The Stage Coach .... Harry Shaw Newman Gallery,
(17″ × 13″) New York, N. Y.

The Shoremen .... W. H. Vodrey,
(13″ × 17″) East Liverpool, O.

Sleigh Ride .... H. N. Harker,
(19″ × 23″) East Liverpool, O.

Soldier Putting on Socks .... Harry O. Eichleay,
(22″ × 26″) Pittsburgh, Pa.

Spilt Milk (Boy Eating Oatmeal) Victor D. Spark,
(The Idiot) (27″ × 22″) New York, N. Y.

Stage Coach..................Duquesne Club,
(17″ × 13″) Pittsburgh, Pa.

Story of the Battle.............Duquesne Club
(25″ × 32″)

Temperance Pledge...........Beverly Wyatt, Inc.,
(15″ × 12″) Pittsburgh, Pa.

Town Crier..................Duquesne Club,
(10″ × 14″) Pittsburgh, Pa.

Truant Boy..................H. N. Harker,
(22″ × 27″) East Liverpool, O.

Trial Scene (Molly Maguire)....Rochester Museum
(27″ × 22″)

Two Urchins in the Pantry......Feragil, Inc.,
(13″ × 11½″) New York, N. Y.

Union Soldier................Heber H. Blythe,
(12″ × 18″) East Liverpool, O.

Union Troops with Hooker.....Harry O. Eichleay,
(21″ × 31½″) Pittsburgh, Pa.

Union Troops Entraining.......Mrs. J. Insley Blair,
(23½″ × 19½″) Tuxedo Park, N. Y.

The Urchin..................Duquesne Club,
(25″ × 30″) Pittsburgh, Pa.

Washerwoman................Harry Shaw Newman Gallery,
(9½″ × 12¼″) New York, N. Y.

Whoa Emma..................Mrs. J. D. Hailman,
(15½″ × 11½″) Pittsburgh, Pa.

Youth......................Mrs. Paul C. Wolff,
(6″ × 10″) Pittsburgh, Pa.

Youth and Sugar Bowl.........Mrs. H. A. Byram,
(22″ × 26″) San Francisco, Calif.

Woodcutter (Clearing the......Harry Shaw Newman Gallery,
Wilderness) (19″ × 26″) New York, N. Y.

The present owners of the following paintings are unknown. Each painting is listed with the name of its owner at the time the last definite record was recorded. Many of these may now be known by other titles.

Abraham Lincoln............. C. W. Batchelor, 1879

The Bum.................... Mary and Cecilia O'Connor, 1932

Conviviality................. Peter Brady, 1859 *(Men Drinking,* now owned by the Historical Society of Western Pennsylvania?)

Cornhusking................. Dr. John Shallenberger, 1879

Court Scene.................. John P. Robitzer, 1879 *(Court Room Scene,* now owned by Mrs. J. Insley Blair?)

Egg Thief.................... James S. Craft, 1860

Emancipation Proclamation.... C. W. Batchelor, 1879 (Lincoln print now in the Library of Congress)

First Shot.................... Henry Miner, 1879

Foreign Loans................ C. W. Batchelor, 1879

Higher Law.................. C. W. Batchelor, 1879

Hopeful Grandson............ Dr. W. M. Wright, 1860

John Brown.................. Rev. R. S. Travelli, 1879

Luxury...................... J. Painter and Sons, 1879

Man Peering from Jail......... Judge Marcus Acheson, 1890

Old Virginia Home............ Joseph H. Davis, 1879

The Painter.................. Alexander Nimick, 1879

Beer Drinker................. D. A. Stewart, 1879 *(Man Drinking* now owned by the Harry Stone Collection?)

Pap Beitler's Roadhouse....... John F. Scott, 1914

Room for Improvement........ D. C. Holmes, 1879

Rustic Courtship.............. Mrs. Isaac Jones, 1879

Schoolmaster................. James Park, Jr., 1879

Secession .... Exhibited in Second Associated Artists, 1860
Sick Headache (pencil) .... John F. Marthens, 1879
Slave Market .... J. C. Thompson, 1914
Slaying the Dragon .... George R. Duncan, 1879 *(Lincoln Slaying the Dragon of the Confederacy?)*
Tagar Whip .... John A. Harper, 1911
Camp Grounds at York .... Capt. M. K. Moorhead, 1895
Young America .... C. H. Wolff, 1860

PORTRAITS PAINTED IN UNIONTOWN IN THE 1840's, PRESUMED DESTROYED

Peter U. Hook
Mrs. Peter U. Hook
William A. West
Mrs. William A. West
John Kimberly
James T. Gorley
William Searight
Mrs. William Searight
John Keffer (known to be destroyed)

CARVINGS

General Lafayette .... Court House, Uniontown, Pa.
Eagle and Beehive .... Horace Frost, Uniontown, Pa.

BIBLIOGRAPHY

The following books, periodicals, and catalogues have been selected either because they have direct references to Blythe and his paintings or because they have discussions of art—painters, style, history—that are closely related to Blythe and help in the understanding and analysis of his art:

Abrahams, Evelyn. "David G. Blythe," in *Antiques,* May 1935.

American Art Union. *Transactions and Bulletins.* New York, 1838-1853.

Ashbee, C. R. *Caricature.* London, 1928.

Baldwin, Leland D. *Pittsburgh: The Story of a City.* Pittsburgh, 1938.

Barth, Harold B. *History of Columbiana County, Ohio.* Indianapolis, 1926. 2 Vols.

Benesch, Otto. *Artistic and Intellectual Trends from Rubens to Daumier.* Cambridge, Mass. 1930.

Benjamin, S. G. W. *Art in America.* New York, 1880.

Biddle, Edward and Fielding, Mantle. *Thomas Sully.* Philadelphia, 1921.

Boswell, Peyton J. *Modern American Painting.* New York, 1940.

Boucher, John Newton. *A Century and a Half of Pittsburgh and Her People.* Pittsburgh, 1908.

Caffin, Charles Henry. *The Story of American Painting.* New York, 1907.

Carnegie Institute. *A Century of American Landscape Painting.* Pittsburgh, 1939.

Christ-Janner, Albert. *George Caleb Bingham of Missouri.* New York, 1940.

Church, Samuel Harden. *A Short History of Pittsburgh 1758-1908.* New York, 1908.

Clark, Edna Marie. *Ohio Art and Artists.* Richmond, Ohio, 1932.

Clayton, Muriel. *The Print Collector.* New York, 1930.

Cortissoz, Royal. *American Artists.* New York, 1923.

Crouse, Russel. *Mr. Currier and Mr. Ives.* New York, 1930.

Dahlinger, Charles W. *Pittsburgh.* New York, 1916.

Dunlap, William. *History of the Rise and Progress of the Arts and Design in the United States.* Boston, 1918. 3 Vols.

Fielding, Mantle. *American Engravers upon Copper and Steel.* Philadelphia, 1917.

Fleming, George Thornton. *History of Pittsburgh and Environs.* New York, 1922. 3 Vols.

———— *Views of Old Pittsburgh.* Pittsburgh, 1932.

Frantz, Henri and Uzanne, Octave. *Daumier and Gavarni.* ed. by Charles Holme. New York, 1904.

Greig, James. *Comic Art in England.* London, 1930.

Hadden, James. *History of Uniontown.* Uniontown, Pa., 1913.

Hagen, Oscar. *The Birth of the American Tradition in Art.* New York, 1940.

Harper, Frank C. *Pittsburgh of Today.* New York, 1931. 4 Vols.

Heilbron, Bertha L. "Making a Motion Picture in 1848," in *Minnesota History: A Quarterly Magazine.* June 1936.

Isham, Samuel. *The History of American Painting.* New York, 1927.

Killikelly, Sarah H. *The History of Pittsburgh.* Pittsburgh, 1906.

Kouwenhoven, John A. *Adventures of America 1857-1900: A Pictorial Record from Harper's Weekly.* New York, 1938.

Lancour, Harold. *American Art Auction Catalogues 1785-1942.* New York, 1944.

Lipman, Jean. *American Primitive Painting.* New York, 1942.

Lynch, Bohem. *A History of Caricature.* London, 1926.

Macartney, Clarence E. *Right Here in Pittsburgh.* Pittsburgh, 1927.

Mather, Frank Jewett. *Estimates in Art.* New York, 1931.

Maurice, Arthur Bartlett and Cooper, Frederic Taber. *The History of the 19th Century in Caricature.* New York, 1904.

McSpadden, Joseph Walker. *Famous Painters of America.* New York, 1907.

Metropolitan Museum of Art. *Life in America.* New York, 1939.

Mott, Frank Luther. *A History of American Magazines 1741-1850.* New York, 1930.

Murrell, William. *A History of American Graphic Humor.* New York, 1933.

Narodny, Ivan. *American Artists.* New York, 1930.

O'Connor, John Jr. "David Gilmour Blythe, Artist," in *Western Pennsylvania Historical Society Magazine,* March-June 1944.

Peters, Harry T. *America on Stone.* New York, 1931.

Pinckney, Pauline A. *American Figureheads and their Carvers.* New York, 1940.

Richardson, Edgar Preston. *American Romantic Painting.* New York, 1944.

——— *The Way of Western Art 1776-1914.* Cambridge, Mass., 1939.

Rourke, Constance. *The Roots of American Culture.* New York, 1942.

Saint-Gaudens, Homer. *The American Artist and his Times.* New York, 1941.

Shackleton, Robert. *Story of Harper's Magazine.* New York, 1916.

Sherman, Frederic Fairchild. *Early American Painting.* New York, 1932.

Simon, Howard. *500 Years of Art and Illustration.* Cleveland, 1942.

Sitwell, Sachaverell. *Narrative Pictures: A Survey of English Genre and its Painters.* London, 1937.

Smith, William Ernest. *The Francis Preston Blair Family in Politics.* New York, 1933.

Stauffer, David McNeely. *American Engravers Upon Copper and Steel.* New York, 1907.

Townsend, F. H. *"Punch" Drawings.* London, 1921.

Walker, John and Magill, James. *Great American Paintings from Smibert to Bellows.* New York, 1943.

Wedmore, Frederick. *The Masters of Genre Painting.* London, 1880.

Weitenkampf, Frank. *American Graphic Art.* New York, 1912.

——— *The Quest of the Print.* New York, 1932.

White, Margaret H. *A Sketch of Chester Harding, Artist, Drawn by his Own Hand.* New York, 1929.

Wilenski, Reginald Howard. *The Modern Movement in Art.* London, 1927.

Whitney Museum of American Art. *American Genre (1800-1935).* New York, 1935.

——— *Blythe-Beale Catalogue of Exhibition April 7-May 7, 1936.* New York, 1936.

Newspapers which contain articles on Blythe and his paintings:

East Liverpool Review. August 22, 1861 and May 26, 1938.

Pittsburgh Commercial Gazette. March 15, 1895—July 15, 1895.

Pittsburgh Daily Post. May 16—July 12, 1865.

Pittsburgh Evening Chronicle. May 15 and 16, 1865.

Pittsburgh Newspaper Abstracts. Collected by Carnegie Library of Pittsburgh, 1942. 20 Vols.

Uniontown News Standard. April 16-20, 1895.

INDEX

THE TEXT
OF THIS BOOK
HAS BEEN SET IN
LINOTYPE CALEDONIA
AND PRINTED ON SPECIAL
WORTHY ALL-RAG PAPER FOR
UNIVERSITY OF PITTSBURGH PRESS
BY DAVIS & WARDE, INC.
ILLUSTRATIONS BY
REPUBLIC PRESS